REFINISHING &
RESTORING YOUR
PIANO

For Carl Kehret, whose talent, expertise and love of old pianos made this book possible.

REFINISHING &
RESTORING YOUR
PIANO

PEG KEHRET

TAB BOOKS Inc.
Blue Ridge Summit, PA 17214

FIRST EDITION

FIRST PRINTING

Copyright © 1985 by TAB BOOKS Inc.

Printed in the United States of America

Reproduction or publication of the content in any manner, without express permission of the publisher, is prohibited. No liability is assumed with respect to the use of the information herein.

Library of Congress Cataloging in Publication Data

Kehret, Peg.
    Refinishing and restoring your piano.

    Includes index.
    1. Piano—Maintenance and repair. I. Title.
ML652.K4   1985   786.2′3   85-4643
ISBN 0-8306-0871-0
ISBN 0-8306-1871-6 (pbk.)

Photography by Robert Bither.

Contents

Introduction

The piano has long been the most popular and widely played musical instrument. Since the first piano was built in 1709, pianos have been enjoyed by amateur and professional musicians alike. During the nineteenth century, a piano in the parlor was the symbol of a gracious home, and most well-bred children received piano lessons.

Many people today still consider piano lessons to be an important part of a child's education. More and more adults are taking lessons, too. Some want to be able to play at parties and sing-alongs; others only want to play privately, for their own personal enjoyment.

Whether a piano is played daily or only occasionally, it is much more than just a musical instrument. It is also a sizable piece of furniture. Unlike a violin or a clarinet, which can be put into a case and tucked out of sight in a closet or cupboard, a piano is in full view 24 hours a day. No matter which room of the house it occupies, it takes up a considerable amount of floor space and is usually one of the focal points of the room.

Because a piano is highly visible, it is logical to want it to be attractive. Yet many homes, which are otherwise tastefully decorated, will have an old upright piano that is nicked, chipped, stained, and scratched. People who wouldn't dream of having a coffee table or end table that was marred by water ring marks from glasses or covered with cigarette burns will keep a piano in exactly that condition. Probably they just don't realize that a piano can be readily refinished, thus vastly improving its appearance and adding substantially to its value.

Refinishing an old piano is a satisfying and profitable project. It requires no special education and no expensive tools. All you need to successfully refinish a piano are simple materials, a willingness to work, and the step-by-step instructions in this book. And, of course, a piano. If you don't already own one that needs refinishing, you will learn how to select a suitable instrument.

You will learn how to take a piano apart, refinish it, and put it back together without harming the inner workings. You will learn how to replace the chipped and missing key covers with new ones, how to cover up nicks and gouges, and how to rejuvenate old pedals.

Even if you have never done any refinishing work before, you will be able to completely refinish your piano for a fraction of what it would cost to have the work done professionally. You won't need to buy any special, hard-to-find tools, and even if you can only work on the project on weekends, you should be able to finish in less than a month.

You will also learn how to use inexpensive solvents instead of high-priced commercial strippers. Most of the commercially marketed products are too expensive for something as large as a piano. Many of them are also too harsh on the fine patina of old wood. When this patina is ruined, the piano loses much of its elegance as well as some of its value. It is possible to do a thorough job of removing the old finish and still preserve the fine patina while using readily available products.

The proper formulas for stripping various piano finishes are included in Chapter 5. These formulas will work well on lacquer, shellac, or varnish and will be gentle on the wood. You will also learn how to apply an elegant new finish to your piano after it has been stripped.

Because most of the older pianos that need refinishing are upright pianos, uprights have been used for the diagrams, photos, and general directions throughout this book. The basic method will work equally well on a baby grand or a grand piano, however.

Refinishing a piano is probably a project that you will do only once in your lifetime; therefore, do it right! Follow the instructions, work carefully, and take pride in your accomplishment.

Chapter 1

Old Piano or New Piano

There are many reasons why it makes sense to fix up an old piano instead of buying a new one. The first reason is obvious—money. Old pianos cost less than new pianos. Even if you figure the dollar value of the time you spend refinishing the instrument, you will probably end up having a smaller investment in an old piano than you would if you went out and bought a new one.

A second good reason to refinish an old piano is uniqueness. The pianos that are manufactured today are well made, sound instruments, but they lack the individual touches that many of the old pianos have. Some of the old instruments have hand carved front panels or hand carving on the legs. Figure 1-1 shows the kind of carving that can be found on older pianos. In today's assembly line kind of manufacturing, there is no place for such elaborate hand carving. In addition, old wood often has a lovely patina that cannot be duplicated in a newer piano no matter how well constructed it is.

An old piano is desirable for the same reasons that fine old furniture pieces are prized by antiques collectors. The style, the wood, the unusual features—these are all attributes that make an old piano valuable simply because it is unique. You cannot order one like it from a catalog or buy its twin at any piano shop.

For many people, there is yet another reason for restoring an old piano—sentiment. Perhaps the piano belonged to Grandma and everyone in the family loved Grandma dearly. They remember

Fig. 1-1. Carving on an old piano.

2

fondly the way she used to practice her scales or play lively tunes at parties. Grandma was a beautiful person, and it would be nice to keep her piano in the family.

Unfortunately, Grandma's piano is not so beautiful. The finish is cracked, blistered, and worn. The keys are chipped, and there are water marks and cigarette burns on the top of the case. It is the one eyesore in an otherwise attractive room.

If you own a family heirloom piano and want to keep it for its sentimental value, you can refinish it and restore it to its former beauty.

Sometimes a piano's value is not so much sentimental as it is practical. Maybe you just like the way your piano plays. Each piano has a different "touch", and when you are used to playing a certain instrument, it is sometimes hard to adjust to a different one. Pianos also have unique tone qualities, and if you like the sound of your old piano, you may never find a newer piano you like as well at any price. In such cases, it makes sense to keep the piano you have. Refinish it, fix it up, give it new keys, if necessary, but keep the basic instrument that you already like and enjoy playing.

Perhaps you don't already own a piano but are looking for one to buy. If so, you may want to consider buying an old piano that needs to be refinished. By doing the work yourself, you will be able to save a tidy sum and will end up with a fine quality instrument. It is quite possible to purchase an old piano and, by spending a few days refinishing it, triple your investment. It is pretty hard to do that well in the stock market. Some pianos have been badly abused by their owners while others need only cosmetic help. If you are willing to spend the time, a mistreated piano can sometimes turn out to be the best buy of all.

A piano technician in Seattle, Washington, tells of buying a baby grand at an auction. The owners had allowed their dog to chew on one of the piano's legs until it was past the point where sanding and refinishing would solve the problem. Even worse, they had spilled a platter of spaghetti with meat sauce on the inside of the piano, all over the strings. Then they poured baking soda on top of the spaghetti sauce in an attempt to neutralize the acid of the tomato. The whole mess had been left to harden.

Needless to say, the bidding at the auction was not spirited. The average piano buyer did not want anything to do with such an instrument, and the technician purchased it for very little. He had to replace the strings, sand and repaint the metal harp, and refinish the entire case. He also paid a cabinetmaker to carve a new leg. It was a lot of time and work, but three months later he sold the baby grand for eight times what he had in it.

That, of course, is an extreme example. You won't find too many pianos full of hardened spaghetti sauce. You will, however, find them with several coats of cracked and peeling paint (including canary yellow, bright pink, and lavender), or a series of rings where glasses have carelessly been set, or a string of cigarette burns.

One man bought an old upright with three bullet holes in the case. On the inside he could see where the bullets had struck the harp, but no damage was done, and the piano sounded fine when it was played. "Because of the bullet holes," he says, "I got the piano cheap. The holes don't affect the sound, and they're a great conversation piece at parties."

There are many pianos with water-marked surfaces, chipped or missing keys, and scratched finishes. Musically, they are perfectly good, but they have low price tags, because they look so terrible. Refinished, such a piano will look just as good as it sounds or even better. If you are willing to spend the time and effort, a piano with a scarred surface can be a real bargain.

Unlike an automobile, which depreciates the minute you drive it away, a piano holds its value for many years. If you buy one that needs work and then fix it up, you are assured of having an instrument whose value exceeds the amount of money you have invested in it.

Monetary value isn't the only thing you will gain from refinishing an old piano. You will also have a solid feeling of personal accomplishment. It is satisfying to take a beat-up looking instrument and turn it into a beautiful piece of furniture.

Few do-it-yourself projects will be as highly visible or produce so many compliments as will a properly refinished piano.

Selecting a Good
Used Piano to Refinish

If you don't already own an old piano and you want to buy one to refinish, you will almost always find a better buy from a private party than you will if you go only to piano dealers. Even those dealers who sell used pianos, and not all of them do, will generally charge more than you will pay for a comparable piano from a private individual. Dealers have overhead; private parties just want to get rid of an unwanted item.

Sometimes people are nervous about buying from a private party because individuals cannot offer warranties or guarantees. If you are careful about the instrument you buy, you need not concern yourself with the lack of a guarantee. Pianos are low maintenance products. If the piano is in good working order when you buy it and if you take proper care of it while you own it, not much is likely to go wrong.

FINDING A USED PIANO

The best place to start looking for a used piano is in the "For Sale" column of the classified section in your local newspaper. Don't overlook the ads in the small weekly papers that are often published in suburban communities. Attend some auctions, too, and stop at garage sales, tag sales, and flea markets.

Let people know that you want to buy an old piano. If you stop at a garage sale, ask the sellers if they happen to have a piano for sale. Even if they don't, their Aunt Mollie might and your interest may be just the prod she needs to get rid of it. It doesn't cost anything to ask.

Another possible source is to call older churches in your area. Sometimes churches, especially those which have been in existence for many years, will have an old piano or two stored in the basement or a back room. A telephone call to the church office is all it takes to motivate the pastor or congregation into selling an unused piano. Such instruments are usually available at a low price because they are not being used anyway. Your call saves the church from having to advertise the piano for sale and the church members are glad to find someone who is willing to haul the instrument away.

Sometimes large department stores that have a piano department will take used pianos in on trade. While these pianos are usually priced higher than you would pay at an auction or from a private party, it's worth checking. If a piano has been taking up floor space for several months, the store may be willing to sell it at a reduced price just to get rid of it, especially if it doesn't look very attractive.

It may take awhile to find the right piano for you, and you will have to spend some time and gasoline driving around to homes, churches, or shops in your area, but if you are persistent, you will be able to find an inexpensive piano with the potential for being beautiful.

RUNNING YOUR OWN AD

Another possible way to find a bargain piano is to run an ad of your own. Make it clear that you are looking for an inexpensive piano and will consider one which is in less than mint condition.

"Family needs older practice piano" makes it clear that you don't expect perfection, and you don't want to pay a lot of money. Or you can say something like, "Wanted: Old piano in need of refinishing. Must have good tone."

One word of caution. If you run a "Want" ad, don't mention price. If you say, "Under $300," or "Will pay up to $300," you may not get as good a bargain as you would get if you didn't mention price at all. The danger is that someone who might have offered his piano for $200, will now ask $300 because he knows you will go that high.

USED PIANO PRICES

How much should you pay? That depends partly on where you

live. Generally, pianos sell for less in the midwest and southern states than they do on the West Coast or East Coast. By reading the ads regularly and looking at a few pianos that are for sale, you will soon get a feeling for prices in your area, and you will be ready to recognize a bargain when you find one.

IS IT WORTH REFINISHING?

A piano of any kind is a big investment, and you will want to be certain that you are spending your hard-earned dollars on an instrument that will remain a solid investment. When you find an old piano for sale, there are several things to look for to be sure it is worth not only the money but also the time that you will be putting into it. A properly refinished piano will be a lovely piece of furniture, but it is still a musical instrument, and before you buy it, you should be sure that its musical parts are in good shape.

If you already own a piano, use these guidelines to determine whether or not it is worth refinishing. You wouldn't paint and rechrome an automobile whose engine was worthless, and you shouldn't strip and refinish a piano unless its musical parts are in good working condition or can be restored to good condition.

POTENTIAL PROBLEMS

Unless a piano has been severely abused, it can usually be brought back to good working order. There are a few problems, however, that you will want to avoid, so it pays to check carefully before you buy.

The Case

First of all, look at the case itself. Do you like the lines? Picture how it would look if you refinished it. Does it have a classic quality or some unique carving that gives it the potential for being truly lovely? If it is a "Plain Jane" piano, and you aren't going to be excited about it even after it is refinished, then it isn't worth your time and work.

Examine the case for signs of damage. You don't need to worry about minor chips, scratches, burns, nicks, or layers of purple paint, because you will be refinishing it anyway. You should worry, however, if the wood is warped or if the sides have been reattached with nails or screws. Look carefully for any signs of termites or rotten wood.

The Sounding Board

Next, look at the sounding board on the back side of the piano (Fig. 2-1). This is the large piece of wood that is visible only from the back side. Sounding boards are usually made of spruce and are about 3/8 inch thick. The purpose of the sounding board is to vibrate, increasing the loudness of the strings.

If the piano has been in extremes of dryness or humidity over the years, the sounding board may be cracked. Small cracks, where the two sides of the crack are still flush, are not serious. A piano can have two or three small cracks in the sounding board and the tonal quality won't be affected. Large cracks, however, are more serious. If the sounding board has any large cracks where space shows between the sides of the crack, you may hear a buzzing or ringing sound when the piano is played. Even large cracks are not necessarily terminal. A sounding board can be shimmed and reglued by a piano technician but such a flaw should be reflected in the purchase price.

Fig. 2-1. A sounding board in good condition.

While you are looking at the back of the piano, check the ribs, which run diagonally across the sounding board. These ribs should not be cracked, and the sounding board should not be pulled away from them. Such damage would indicate that the piano may have been dropped, and, if so, you will want to avoid it.

Figure 2-1 shows a sounding board in good condition. There are no cracks, and the ribs are not loose. Figure 2-2 shows a rib which has come loose from the sounding board; note the small gap of space between the sounding board itself and the rib.

Another way to check the sounding board is to remove the front bottom panel of the piano and shine a flashlight behind the strings. This lets you check the front side of the sounding board for cracks. Small cracks, where the two sides of the crack are still flush, are not serious. You only need to be concerned about large cracks where space shows between the sides of the crack.

The Tuning Pins

Another potential problem with an old piano is loose tuning pins. The tuning pins are what the top ends of the piano strings are wound around. As the name implies, these pins are tightened or loosened to change the tautness of the strings. By controlling the tautness of the strings, you control the pitch of the individual notes. If a tuning pin is turned clockwise, it makes the string tighter and the sound of the note higher. If it is turned counterclockwise, it loosens the string and makes the tone of the note lower. If the tuning pins on a piano are loose, the piano will not stay in tune.

The best way to tell if the tuning pins are loose is to play the piano an octave (12 notes) at a time. That is, play the bottom C and the C above it at the same time. Then play the bottom C# and the C# above it. Progress up the keys, each time playing two notes an octave apart. The notes should sound the same. Even if the piano is out of tune, which it probably will be, the notes should be uniformly out of tune.

If you play two notes an octave apart and they sound far apart in tone, chances are you have a loose tuning pin. Loose tuning pins will need the attention of a piano technician before the piano will hold its tune. If you suspect loose tuning pins, contact a piano technician and find out how much it would cost to have the work done.

The Hammers

Look down inside the piano and check the hammers. They are

Fig. 2-2. A sounding board with a loose rib.

easy to find. There will be a whole row (one for each note of your piano) of wooden sticks, each with a rounded felt head. It is this head that actually touches the string when you play a note on the piano. Figure 2-3 shows a new piano hammer. Play a note and watch the action of the hammer, and you will see that this part of the piano is aptly named.

Examine the front edges of the felt, where the hammers strike the strings. Any piano that has been played much will show some wear on the hammers, but when hammers are grooved too deeply, they pluck the strings instead of hitting them. The hammers on some old pianos are actually worn through to the wooden core. If the groove in the hammers is 1/8 inch deep or more, the hammers may need to be replaced before the piano will have a good tone. Moderately grooved hammers won't damage the piano, so if the hammers are only somewhat grooved but the sound is still pleasing to you, it isn't necessary to replace the hammers.

In Fig. 2-4, the top hammer is new. The center hammer is slightly worn with shallow grooves. This would still be acceptable. The bottom hammer shows excessive wear. The front edge is flattened, and there are deep groves. Hammers with this kind of wear would need to be replaced.

While you are checking the hammer heads for grooves, make sure they haven't been eaten by moths or mice. In Fig. 2-5, the rounded heads of the hammers on the left have been completely eaten away by mice. Note the tuft of felt that was chewed off but left behind on the center hammer.

In addition to the felt heads, the hammers may have problems with the wooden shanks. If some of the wooden shanks are broken, those notes won't play. Look down inside to see if the broken hammers are lying there ready to be glued back in. If not, it still isn't too serious. One possible inexpensive remedy if you have only one or two broken shanks is to replace the broken ones with complete hammers from the highest or lowest notes on the keyboard. This can be done if the hammers that are broken are the same size as the high or low hammers. These very high or very low notes are hardly ever played anyway so if they don't work, it won't make much difference. The other alternative is to have a piano technician replace any broken hammers. This is a simple and inexpensive solution.

The Strings

While you are looking inside the piano, examine the strings.

Fig. 2-3. A new piano hammer.

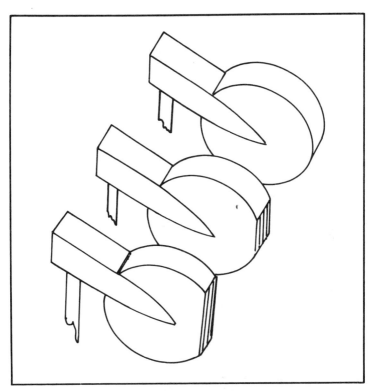

Fig. 2-4. From the top: new hammer, hammer with moderate wear, a badly worn hammer.

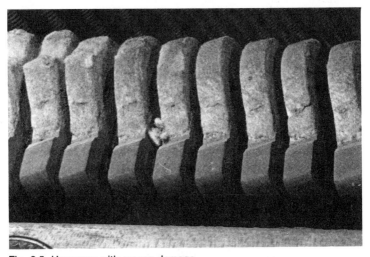

Fig. 2-5. Hammers with mouse damage.

13

Don't touch them because the natural oil on your fingers will cause the strings to corrode. Are the strings all there? The bottom 12 notes of a piano usually have one string per key. These are the bass strings. The next octave will have two strings for each key. The rest of the piano will have three strings per key. This may vary, but you will easily be able to tell if any of the strings are broken or missing, because there will be a gap in the otherwise uniformly spaced strings. A piano tuner can replace strings quickly at minimal cost.

Look to see if the strings are rusty. An accumulation of rust on the strings and tuning pins is an indication that the piano has been in a damp environment for a long time. If this is the case, get your nose into the act and smell the inside of the piano for mildew. A strong, musty odor, indicating mildew, is hard to correct.

Missing or Broken Keys

Don't worry if the keys are chipped or the covers are missing. Replacing either white or black key covers is a simple, inexpensive task, which you can do yourself. Chapter 6 tells you how.

THE PIANO'S AGE AND MANUFACTURER

You will probably be curious about the age and make of the piano. There may be a stencil on the front of the piano giving the maker's name and possibly the city where the piano was manufactured. If not, the name of the manufacturer can usually be found on the inside of the piano.

Lift cover of the piano and look inside. You will see a large metal harp covering most of the width of the piano at the top end. The tuning pins will be attached to this harp and the strings will be covering it. Many times, the manufacturer's name will be in raised letters,molded into the top of this harp. The manufacturer of the piano in Fig. 2-6 is the A. M. McPhail Co. of Boston.

Don't be concerned if you don't recognize the name of the manufacturer. Brand names can be confusing because there are more than 5,000 brands of pianos. Some piano manufacturers make more than one brand name of piano. Many companies have been bought out by other companies over the years. The Kohler and Campbell Company, which began in 1896, has manufactured pianos under dozens of different names, including Astor, Frances Bacon, Behr Brothers, McPhail, Preston, Triumph, and Waldorf. The Aeolian-American Corporation is the consolidation of the American

Fig. 2-6. Manufacturer's name on the harp.

Piano Company and the Aeolian Company. Among others, this firm makes Brewster, Chickering, Mason & Hamlin, Knabe, Stuyvesant, and Chilton pianos.

In addition to such large, well-known companies, there are many fine smaller manufacturers. Depending on the age of your piano, the maker may or may not still be in business. Because piano parts are almost universally standardized, the availability of parts is not a problem even for pianos whose makers are no longer in business.

Many pianos will name the city where they were made as well as the manufacturer. This information is often right on the front of the piano. If not, it might be found on the harp, next to the manufacturer's name or even on the back on the sounding board. Check to see if it was made in the United States or in Europe. In recent years, many old pianos have been imported from England and other European countries. Some of these are fine instruments; some are not.

Many of the European pianos have what is called a "birdcage" action, which makes them hard to tune, and requires more frequent tuning. Some piano tuners prefer not to work on pianos that have a birdcage type action. If the piano you are considering is a European make, you may want to get the opinion of a good piano tuner before you buy it.

American made pianos generally have a standard action (Fig. 2-7). Once they are restored to good condition, such a piano will usually hold a tune well.

To determine the age of a piano, it is necessary to locate the serial number. Usually this will be a six-digit number. On grand pianos, the serial number is always on the harp, either on the far left or far right at the keyboard end or approximately in the center. In order to see the serial number on a grand piano, the sliding music rack will need to be pulled forward and off the piano. On upright pianos, the serial number is usually burned or engraved in the wood near the manufacturer's name on the inside. Sometimes it is located on the harp. The serial number of the piano in Fig. 2-6 is on the harp in between the tuning pins for the bass strings and the tuning pins for the treble strings, just above the shield-shaped decal. Sometimes the serial number is printed on the wood case (Fig. 2-8) on the back side of the piano near the top.

Write down the name of the manufacturer, exactly as it appears on the piano, and the serial number. Most libraries have reference books that will enable you to look up the age of the piano.

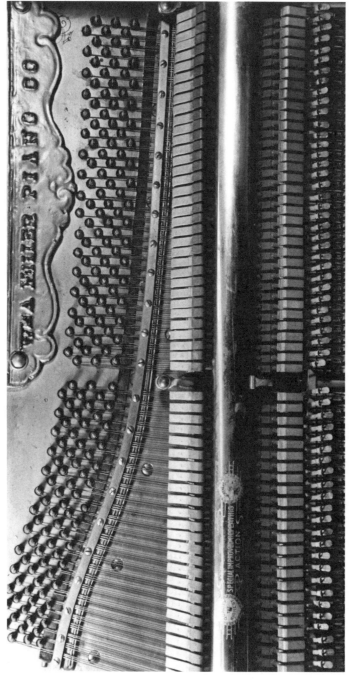

Fig. 2-7. A standard action such as is in most American-made pianos.

Fig. 2-8. Serial number on the back of the case.

One good reference source is the *Pierce Piano Atlas,* published by Bob Pierce, 1880 Termino, Long Beach, CA 90815. This book is available in most libraries and is updated regularly. It lists piano manufacturers alphabetically and gives pertinent information about each, such as whether the company is still in business, and, if not, who bought them out. Under each manufacturer's name, there is a list of serial numbers of the pianos and the dates they were made. For example, under Chickering & Sons, you learn that serial numbers 126000 to 127500 were manufactured in 1916.

Of course, it isn't necessary to know either the manufacturer or the age of your piano in order to enjoy the instrument. Such information is only to satisfy the owner's curiosity. Condition is far more important than age.

OTHER FACTORS TO CONSIDER

There are many other factors to consider before purchasing a piano.

Size

Before you buy a piano, you should measure it to be sure it will fit in the spot where you want to put it. Besides measuring the space where it will stand, be sure you can get it through your doors and around any necessary corners. Many old pianos are BIG.

Tone

If the piano's condition seems to be good, play it and listen to how it sounds. if you don't know how to play, take along a friend who does or ask the sellers to play it for you. You cannot judge the tone of a piano simply by going up and down the scales with one finger. You should hear a song or two.

You don't need to be a trained musician to know if a particular piano is pleasing to your ear. Naturally, it won't sound as good now as it will when you are done with it. Some notes may not play at all, and it will almost certainly need tuning. Still, you should like the overall tone quality of any piano you buy. If it seems flat and dull or has a tinny, honky-tonk sound, you will want to continue your search elsewhere.

Touch

You should also be satisfied with the touch; that is, the keys should not press down too hard nor should they be overly loose. Stiff actions, where the keys must be pressed hard before they work, are more common than loose ones.

Playing a piano with a stiff touch is much like typing on a manual typewriter. Playing a piano with a light touch is like using an electric typewriter. The touch doesn't affect the tone, only the feel of the keys. Some people swear by an old manual typewriter while others wouldn't trade their IBM Selectric for anything. It is the same way with pianists. Some like a stiff touch, some want it light. Touch is a matter of individual preference so as long as you are happy with it, it doesn't make any difference whether it is on the stiff side or has a light touch. Just be sure you like what you are buying.

Finish

One other fact to consider when purchasing an old piano is what kind of finish the piano has now. If the piano has its original finish, usually lacquer or shellac, it will be easier to strip than if the piano has been painted. Pianos that have been painted or antiqued can still be stripped, but it will take longer than if the piano still has its original finish, and it will require the use of more costly stripping materials.

Bench

Ask if there is a bench or stool that goes with the piano. Often people who are selling a piano will be using the bench or stool in a different part of their house, and if you don't ask for it, they will forget to give it to you. If there isn't a bench or stool, you will need to get one.

MOVING A PIANO

Once you have decided on a piano and have agreed on a price, you are faced with the problem of getting it to your own home. You can, of course, hire a piano mover to do the job for you. They are fast, efficient, and usually expensive. If the piano has to go up or down many stairs, it may be worth the money required to hire professional piano movers.

The alternative is to move it yourself. If you decide to do it yourself, be sure to get enough help. It will take a minimum of four strong adults. You will also need a truck with a ramp. A pick-up truck is okay, but it must have a ramp to get the piano up and down. There is no way to safely lift a heavy piano 3 feet straight up. If you don't have a ramp, you can make a temporary one out of a sheet of 3/4-inch plywood resting on top of two 4- x -4s spaced 2 feet apart.

It is possible to rent a truck that has a hydraulic lift. Then all you have to do is get the piano on the lift, and it will be raised up into the truck. You will still need help to be sure the piano is properly balanced and to get it on the lift.

You will also need a mover's dolly, which can be rented. Many old pianos have wheels on them. These are only casters; they are fine for pushing the piano away from the wall in order to vacuum behind it, but they are usually not adequate for rolling the instrument out of the house and up the ramp to the truck. Pianos are heavy, but they are also fragile, and the last thing you want to do is to tip over while you are moving it. Piano dollys are available at most rental supply houses and will make your job both easier and safer.

Once the piano is on the front of the truck, push it up against the front end as close as you can and TIE IT DOWN SECURELY. Never drive away with a piano that isn't securely tied down with heavy rope. Go slowly around all corners. Even though a piano is heavy, it will tip over very easily if it isn't securely tied. When you get home, use the ramp and the dolly to move the piano to wherever you are going to work on it.

TAKE A BEFORE PICTURE

At this time, you may want to take a "before" picture of your piano. Later, when your refinishing job is done, you will enjoy comparing this before picture with the beautiful, finished piano.

PIANO CHECKLIST

Here is a convenient checklist which outlines the main points to look for when you are examining a piano. You will find this checklist handy to use when you are shopping for a piano to refinish.

1. SOUNDING BOARD
   - ☐ No cracks large enough to see light through.
   - ☐ No more than three small cracks.
   - ☐ Ribs not cracked or pulled loose.
2. TUNING PINS
   - ☐ Play piano by octaves: listen for uniformity of tone.
3. HAMMERS
   - ☐ How many missing?
   - ☐ Grooves no more than 1/8-inch deep.
4. STRINGS
   - ☐ Are they all there?
   - ☐ Are they rusty?
5. CASE
   - ☐ Is the wood warped?
   - ☐ Is there a musty smell?
   - ☐ Is there any damage to indicate the piano has been dropped?
   - ☐ Do you like the style?
6. MANUFACTURER
   - ☐ Is the piano American or European?
   - ☐ Standard action?
   - ☐ Check serial number to find out age.
7. SIZE
   - ☐ Measure to be sure the piano will fit your space.
8. SOUND
   - ☐ Play a song. Is the tone pleasing?
   - ☐ Check the touch; be sure it isn't too hard to play.
9. SEAT
   - ☐ Does a bench or stool come with the piano?

Getting Started

When following the instructions in this book, read each section all the way through before you start to work. Then go back and follow the instructions. For example, when you are ready to remove the keys, read all of the material under "Removing the Keys" in Chapter 4 before you do anything. Then go back and follow the directions, one step at a time.

When you remove the pieces of the piano, all of the pieces that you mark "left" or "right" should be marked as if you are facing the piano. That is, the left leg is the one on your left as you stand in front of the keyboard facing the piano.

WORK SPACE

The first thing you must have when you begin the job of refinishing your piano is space. Not only will you need an adequate, well-ventilated work space, you will also need some storage area where you can keep the keys, key frame, and action of the piano during the refinishing process.

It isn't necessary for the work area and the storage area to be the same, but it is important that the inner parts of the piano be safely stored where they won't be bumped, knocked over, or otherwise disturbed while you are stripping and refinishing the case.

EQUIPMENT AND MATERIALS NEEDED

The following is a list of equipment and materials you will need.

You should assemble as many of these as possible in advance. Once you start work on the piano, you won't want to keep stopping to go after supplies.

- ☐ Vacuum cleaner.
- ☐ Soft paint brush, 1-1 1/2 inches wide. This can be an old paint brush as long as the bristles are still soft.
- ☐ Screwdrivers. You will need two sizes—one for large screws and one for small screws.
- ☐ Small Crescent wrench or open end wrench.
- ☐ 0000 steel wool (very fine).
- ☐ Masking tape, any width.
- ☐ Wooden sticks, such as those used in ice cream bars and Popsicles. (These are not mandatory, but they are useful.)
- ☐ Two fibrous all-purpose cleaning pads. These all-purpose cleaning and finishing pads are usually green and are approximately 6 by 9 inches in size. Bear-Tex is one brand; Stripper's Mate is another. There is an all-purpose cleaning pad in Fig. 3-1, underneath the two calipers and the screw gauge.
- ☐ Two sheets of plastic film, each should be at least 5 feet square. Black plastic is available at most hardware stores and nurseries.
- ☐ Staple gun if possible. If you don't already own a staple gun, you don't have to buy one; you can use thumb tacks.
- ☐ One gallon of lacquer thinner (not necessary if piano has been painted).
- ☐ One gallon of denatured alcohol or shellac thinner (not necessary if piano has been painted).
- ☐ Screw gauge. This is a slotted piece of sheet metal that lets you measure the diameter of screws. The screw gauge in Fig. 3-1 is in the center of the all-purpose cleaning pad, and there is a closer view of a screw gauge in Fig. 3-6 and 3-7. If you don't own a screw gauge, you should borrow or buy one for this project.
- ☐ Paper and pencil.
- ☐ Large pan, approximately 18 by 24 by 6 inches. This is also a must. You can use a large dishpan (sometimes extra big ones are available at restaurant supply houses) or a sturdy cat litter pan.
- ☐ Small, stiff scrub brush or an old toothbrush.
- ☐ Empty coffee cans with lids or similar containers.

- [ ] Lots of absorbent rags.
- [ ] Caliper or small, accurate ruler.
- [ ] Paper cups or other small containers such as empty cottage cheese or margarine cartons. You will need at least a dozen.
- [ ] Rubber gloves.
- [ ] Cotton garden gloves.
- [ ] Four pieces of 4-×-4 lumber. Each piece should be 8-16 inches long.
- [ ] Paint roller pan.
- [ ] Friends. You will need them to help you lift occasionally.
- [ ] Pocket knife. This is not mandatory, but it is useful.
- [ ] Mallet. Again, this is not mandatory, but if you have one, you will probably use it.
- [ ] Old iron (necessary if you are going to replace the key covers or put new veneer on the key blocks).
- [ ] Four gallons of paint stripper. This is necessary <u>only</u> if your piano has been painted. Don't buy it otherwise.
- [ ] Can of WD-40.
- [ ] White glue.
- [ ] Contact cement.
- [ ] Old newspapers.

Figure 3-1 shows some of the supplies you will need. From the left, in the photo, you see: TOP—rubber gloves, paper cups and empty containers, wooden sticks, 0000 steel wool, and Crescent wrench. BOTTOM—staple gun, screw-drivers, caliper, screw gauge, a different kind of caliper, pocket knife, chisel, paint brush, and mallet. The two calipers and the screw gauge are on top of an all-purpose cleaning pad.

ORDERING NEW KEY COVERS

You need to decide if you want to replace the key covers, white or black. The black key covers don't usually need to be replaced, but the white ones frequently do.

Sometimes so many of the white key covers are missing that it is imperative to replace them (Fig. 3-2). Other times, the key covers are all there but some are badly chipped (Fig. 3-3). Pianos such as these will look much better with new white key covers. Replacing the covers is not difficult; full instructions are in Chapter 6.

Most key covers today are made of plastic. It is possible to pur-

Fig. 3-1. Some of the tools and supplies needed.

25

Fig. 3-2. Many white key covers missing.

chase new ivory key covers, but they cost approximately ten times more than the plastic ones. Some people prefer ivory key covers no matter how expensive they are. Some manufacturers make simulated ivory key covers. These are plastic covers with a

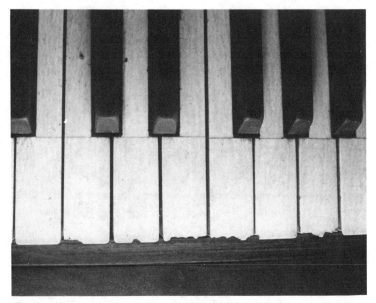

Fig. 3-3. Chipped keys.

marbleized grain. Most people don't care what the keys are made of so long as they look nice. Contrary to what you may have heard, ivory keys do not add substantially to the value of a piano.

Figure 3-4 shows a piano with new white plastic key covers. Key covers are also sometimes called key tops or key facings. There are two types of white key covers available. One type has two pieces for each key—a top and a front. The second kind is all in one piece with the front already attached to the top. This second kind, where the front and top are attached, is much easier to put on the keys and will have more uniform appearance.

ORDER A CATALOG OF PIANO PARTS

Whether or not you intend to replace the key covers, you should order a catalog of piano parts. Both white and black key covers are available by mail, and there are a few other small parts that you will probably need to replace as you go along. It will be easier to do if you have a piano catalog.

Order your catalog now so that it will arrive by the time you are ready to order your new covers and/or other small parts. There are several mail order sources for new key covers and other piano parts. Among them are The Player Piano Co., Schaff Piano Supply Co., and Pacific Piano Supply Co. The addresses and telephone numbers of these companies are in the suppliers list found in the

Fig. 3-4. New white plastic key covers.

Appendix. You may call or write them for a catalog; there will usually be a small charge for sending it.

As you take your piano apart, keep a list of items that need to be replaced. If you intend to put on new key covers, put key covers first on your list of parts to be ordered.

MOVING PIANO TO WORK AREA

After you have gathered your supplies, you can move the piano to the area where you will be stripping it if it isn't already there. This area must have plenty of space and good ventilation. A garage is often a good choice, or, if climate permits, a covered patio. You will want to protect the floor of your work space from splatters and splashes, so put several thicknesses of old newspaper on the floor before you move the piano in.

Most pianos roll fairly easily across the floor on their casters if you don't have too far to go. If you will be going across flagstone, put down newspapers or an old rug because casters tend to scratch flagstone. If you must go up or down any steps, even just one or two, be sure you get enough help. If the piano has to go up or down several steps, you should rent a piano dolly.

TAKING THE PIANO APART

You are now ready to begin taking your piano apart. Taking the piano apart enables you to strip each individual piece separately and completely. You will be able to do a more thorough job of stripping, and it will be far easier to handle the pieces one at a time.

Trying to save time by stripping a piano without taking it apart will almost always result in an unsatisfactory job. It is not uncommon to find partially stripped pianos for sale. Invariably, the owners tried to strip the piano intact and then got so discouraged that they quit part way through and put the instrument up for sale. (At a bargain price, half-stripped pianos are not particularly attractive.)

It is actually less work and will take less time to strip a piano if it is taken apart first than it will if it is done in one piece. The end result will be better, too. For example, stripping one piano leg according to the instructions in this book is an easy task. One end of the leg rests in a large pan of stripper so drips are easily controlled. As you work, you can readily turn the leg to get at all sides. If there are carvings or grooves, you can easily reach them. When one end is done, it is a simple matter to turn the leg over and work on the other end. The top of the leg, where it joins the rest of the piano, is totally accessible. You don't have to worry about splashing stripper on other parts of the case that are already done.

By contrast, imagine trying to strip a piano leg that is still attached to the piano. You can't lift the leg or turn it. It is hard to even see the back side at the top where it joins the rest of the piano. Drips and splashes are hard to control, and it is extremely difficult to get all the old finish removed, especially if there are any grooves or carvings.

If you think the legs would be hard, imaging trying to strip the front panel while it is still attached. Where does the gooey stripper go—down between the keys, or into the inside of the piano to corrode the action? Fortunately, you don't have to worry about such problems, because you will be taking your piano apart before you start to strip it.

It is imperative to remove all the old finish if the piano is going to look good when it is done. In order to do this, you must be able to get at the crevices and the ends of the pieces where they join together. These hard-to-reach places are almost impossible to do when the piano is in one piece. The time you spend disassembling the piano and putting it back together will pay big dividends in the look of the finished product.

Once you begin refinishing your piano, you will want to work at it as steadily as you can until it is finished. Don't begin if you know you have only one free evening and then won't be able to continue the job until next month. Working steadily will help you remember which parts go where. Even though you will be keeping careful records as you take your piano apart, it is always easier to reassemble a piano when not much time has elapsed since it was taken apart.

Piano Parts

As you work, you will need to become familiar with the names of the various parts of the piano (Fig. 3-5). You will find it handy to insert a bookmark at Fig. 3-5 so that you can readily refer back to it as you work.

You might also want to take some snapshots as you disassemble the piano. This isn't imperative since you will be diagramming your work, but for some people photos are an extra, easy way to refresh their memories about exactly which piece went where. Shooting a roll of film as you work is cheap insurance and the pictures, like your "before" picture, will make good conversation later.

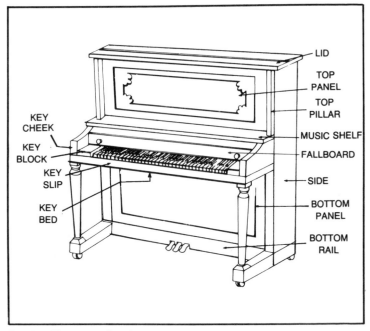

Fig. 3-5. The parts of a piano.

Measure and Mark Every Screw

During the disassembly, you will need to measure each screw as soon as you take it out, both for diameter and for length. <u>This is essential.</u>

To do this accurately, you should use a screw gauge. Figure 3-6 shows how to measure the length of a screw using a screw gauge. The screw in Fig. 3-6 is 2 3/4 inches long. Figure 3-7 shows how to measure a screw's diameter with a screw gauge. The screw in Fig. 3-7 is a #10 screw.

Make a rough sketch of each piece of the piano that you remove and write on your sketch the location and size of each screw. You will need to do this with every screw on every piece you take apart. When it is time to put the piano together again, you will want to replace each screw in the same hole it came out of. In order to do this, you must keep track of the screws according to which piece they were in and where. After you have marked the location and size of the screws on your sketch, put the screws in a paper cup and mark the cup with the name of the piece that they came out of.

Some pieces of the piano will have several pieces of hardware or more than one size of screw. Be sure to make a detailed sketch

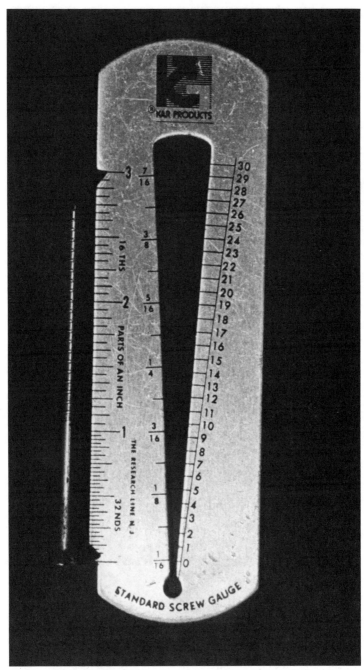

Fig. 3-6. Measuring the length of a screw using a screw gauge.

31

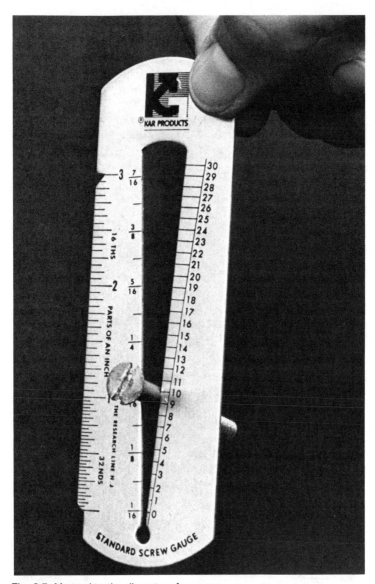

Fig. 3-7. Measuring the diameter of a screw.

of such pieces. Besides marking screw location and size on the sketch, write down where the screws are stored. Figure 3-8 shows a sketch of the back side of a top panel. Notice that the worker's notes to himself indicate where the various screws are stored, such as "in cup marked pivot."

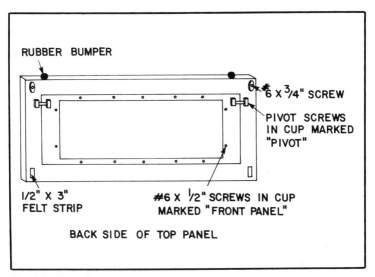

Fig. 3-8. Worker's diagram of a top panel.

If you keep records of this kind as the piano is disassembled, you will have no trouble getting each screw back into the proper hole when it is time to put the refinished piano back together. The importance of this cannot be stressed too much.

Don't try to trust your memory. If you don't mark the screws and their locations properly, it is easy to get mixed up. You might use the right diameter screw but the wrong length. If you use a screw that's too long, it can damage the piece into which it is inserted. If the screw is too short, it won't hold properly. So don't take chances. Measure and mark each screw as you remove it.

You can also write the screw size in pencil on the back of the piano piece next to the hole it came out of. It is helpful to do this when there are two identical pieces, such as the Left Top Pillar and the Right Top Pillar. Be sure to press firmly with your pencil so your mark makes a slight indentation. On flat pieces, which have only one or two screws, it may be faster to write the screw sizes on the back of the piece than it is to make a sketch. Be sure, however, to keep track of the screws by poking them through a piece of paper that's labeled with the name of the piano piece. Some pieces, such as the long hinge across the top of the piano and the hinge on the fallboard, which comes down over the keys, may have several identical screws all in a row. In these cases, you don't need to make a sketch or number the screws, just put all the screws into a paper cup and label the cup "Top Hinge" or "Fallboard Hinge."

Top Panel Removal

To begin the disassembly, lift the top lid of the piano and look inside. At the back side of the top panel on each end, there will be some type of mechanism that secures the top panel to the piano. On some pianos, the top panel tips forward, forming a music rack, when the key cover is raised. On this kind of piano, there will be some sort of pivot point at each end of the top panel. It may be a hinge or merely pins in either end of the top panel. On other pianos, the top panel is stationary. In these cases, there will usually be a hook and eye securing the top panel to the piano.

Release whatever is securing the top panel and carefully remove the top panel from the piano (Fig. 3-9). If it isn't obvious which is the top and which is the bottom of the top panel, mark the backside in pencil with an arrow indicating up. Be sure to press firmly enough to make an indentation; otherwise, the mark might accidentally be rubbed off or removed by stripper.

When you have the top panel off, remove from it any individual pieces of hardware such as a hinge or latch. Store each of these and its screws in a separate plastic bag or paper cup along with a note saying exactly where they belong on the piano. For example: "hinge and screws from top panel, bottom left corner." Be sure to use a separate container for each piece of hardware.

Top Pillars Removal

On each side of the piano, next to where the sides of the top panel were, you will find the top pillars (Fig. 3-5.) If these top pillars are screwed on, you should remove them. Look at the pillars on the inside, both from the side and from the rear. If there are screws, you will be able to see them. Figure 3-10 shows a right top pillar being removed. Note the location of the screws.

If your top pillars are screwed on, remove the screws. As you remove each one, measure it and write its size—in pencil—next to the screw hole on the backside of the pillar. Put the screws in a paper cup marked "right top pillar" or "left top pillar."

As you remove each pillar, mark it on the backside: "L" for left pillar or "R" for right pillar and put an arrow indicating up. Figure 3-11 shows the screw size, has an arrow for up, and is marked R for right. Whenever you have two identical pieces or a piece that doesn't have an obvious top and bottom, you should put this kind of description on the backside.

Sometimes the top pillars are glued on. In these cases, there

Fig. 3-9. Removing the top panel.

will be no screws, and the top pillars will have to stay where they are. The purpose of removing them, when possible, is to make it easier to strip them properly. If they are glued on, they will have to be stripped as part of the side of the piano.

Music Shelf Removal

The next piece to come off is the music shelf. This is a board that runs the width of the piano and that the music sits on. The

Fig. 3-10. Removing the right top pillar.

music shelf also acts as a cover for the fallboard. If in doubt about which part is which, refer back to Fig. 3-5.

Usually, there will be a screw at each end of the music shelf holding it down. Make a sketch of the music shelf. Remove the

Fig. 3-11. Marking the back of a right top pillar.

screws, measure them, and write the sizes on your sketch. Also write the screw number on your sketch and a matching number on the piece of paper that you poke the screw through. Be sure to mark the paper "music shelf."

Now, lift the music shelf up and out (Fig. 3-12). If yours won't lift straight up, try sliding it forward toward you. Occasionally, there is a guide on the bottom side of the music shelf.

After you have taken off the top panel, top pillars, and music shelf, the playing mechanism or action of the piano will be exposed. As you work, take care not to bump the hammers or other parts of the action.

Fallboard Removal

Now close the fallboard completely over the keys. On the backside of the fallboard, there will be a screw at each end attaching the fallboard to the backside of the key blocks. Remove these two screws and put them in a paper cup marked "fallboard." The fallboard will now lift up and off the piano (Fig. 3-13).

After you have the fallboard off, label it "fallboard" with a piece of masking tape. You cannot write with your pencil on the fallboard because both sides are visible and will be refinished. So label it with tape and set it aside. You will be dismantling the fallboard more completely later on.

Bottom Panel Removal

Next remove the bottom panel. There is usually a latch at the top of the bottom panel. Undo this latch and tilt the top of the panel toward you about 6 inches. Remove it by lifting it up and off the wooden dowels (Fig. 3-14). When you have the bottom panel off, mark it "bottom panel" on the backside with your pencil. If necessary, also mark an arrow to indicate up.

How the Pedal Dowels Work

It is almost time to remove the action itself. Before you do, get down on your knees and push on the right hand pedal with your hand. On the left side of the piano, you will see a wooden dowel, about 5/8 inch in diameter, which is connected to the back of this pedal. When you push on the pedal, the dowel moves and makes the dampers move away from the strings. The pedal dowels are connected to the pedals by the rocker arms. Figure 3-15 shows two

Fig. 3-12. Removing the music shelf.

Fig. 3-13. Removing the fallboard.

rocker arms and two pedal dowels. It also illustrates how the pedal dowels are connected to the action.

Push the pedal up and down a few times to see exactly how it works. Next push down on the left pedal with your hand. There will be a dowel connected to it, also. This dowel will move the hammers forward toward the strings. If there is a center pedal, push it, too.

It is important to know exactly where these dowels are because as you lift the action out of the piano, the dowels will come loose and you will need to know where they belong. Make a sketch or take a photograph of the top and bottom of each pedal dowel.

Notice also how the dampers are positioned on the strings. Usually there are 10 single strings on the bottom or left-hand end of the piano. The dampers for these strings are U-shaped and rest around the strings. The next 16 notes have two strings. The dampers for these are V-shaped and slip in between the two strings. The rest of the piano notes have three strings. These dampers are flat and cover all three strings. It is important to be familiar with exactly how the dampers are positioned so that when it is time to put the action back in your piano, you will get the dampers the way they are supposed to be. Make some notes to yourself.

Action Removal

After you feel familiar with the pedal dowels and how they work, it is time to remove the action. Usually, there are four or more bolts with knurled knobs, which secure the action to the harp. Refer back to Fig. 2-7; you can see these knurled knobs just above the hammers on the far right and in the center of the picture. Remove these knobs but <u>do not</u> remove the bolts. The knobs are interchangeable so you don't need to keep them in order. Put them in a paper cup labeled "knobs for action bolts."

It will take two people to lift the action our of the piano, not because it is heavy, but because it must be lifted carefully so as not to damage any of the parts. Don't try to do it alone.

Have one person stand at each end of the action where the bolts attached it to the harp. Hold on to the metal frame of the action and gently tilt the top of the action forward about 2 inches so that the dampers no longer make any contact with the strings. Carefully lift the action up and out of the piano (Fig. 3-16). The pedal dowels may want to come along. They should be pulled loose from the action and left where they are if possible. If they cannot by pulled loose, take them out attached to the action, but be sure to note which

Fig. 3-14. Removing the bottom panel.

holes in the key bed they came out of. If you are taking photographs as you go, this would be a good time to take one. As you and your helper lift the action up and out, have a third person snap the picture.

Remember not to touch the piano strings with your fingers. The natural acids from your hands will corrode the strings.

Some actions can be set on the floor, and they are stable enough to stand up by themselves. Other actions cannot stand alone and

Fig. 3-15. The pedal dowels and rocker arms.

Fig. 3-16. Removing the action.

44

Fig. 3-17. Cleaning the action with a reverse vacuum.

will need to be carefully propped up so there is no chance of them falling over. Do not lay the action down as there is too great a risk of bending or smashing a part.

When the action is on the floor, look down into it. Below the rounded hammer heads at the bottom end of the hammer shanks you will see many small springs. They are particularly visible at the upper- or right-hand end of the action. These springs work in conjunction with the hammers and dampers and must not be bent, broken, or pushed out of the slots they rest in.

Cleaning the Action

If the action looks dirty, this is the time to clean it. The best way to clean the action is with a vacuum cleaner that will reverse and blow air. Carefully carry the action outside, and, using the reverse vacuum as a blower, blow the dust off the action without actually touching the action itself (Fig. 3-17). Be careful not to let the end of the vacuum come in contact with the action as there are many small pieces that could be bent, broken, or put out of line. If you don't have a reverse vacuum, you can use a large diameter soda straw to blow much of the dust out of the action. This takes a little longer, but it does an adequate job of cleaning the action. Again, be careful not to let the end of the straw touch the action.

When the action has been cleaned, it should be put in the storage area where it will be safe for the duration of the refinishing process.

Chapter 4

Disassembling the
Rest of the Piano

As you take the rest of the piano apart, continue to measure and mark the screws and to make sketches of the parts and where they belong. Remember, the more careful you are about keeping records now, the easier it will be when you put the piano back together.

REMOVING THE PEDAL DOWELS

Take out the pedal dowels by lifting them up and out (Fig. 4-1). Mark the dowels "front" and "rear" so you will be able to get them back in the proper holes later. Also, mark the rocker arms that the pedal dowels are attached to at the bottom of the piano "front" and "rear."

REMOVING THE KEY SLIP

Next, remove the key slip. This is the piece you see across the front of the piano, directly below the keys (See Fig. 3-5). Usually there are three or four screws coming up from the bottom of the piano through the key bed and into the bottom of the key slip. Get down on your hands and knees and look up at the bottom of the key slip and you will see these screws. Remove these screws (Fig. 4-2) and mark their location and size on a sketch or on the bottom of the key slip.

REMOVING THE KEYS

When the key slip has been removed, all of the keys should

Fig. 4-1. Removing a pedal dowel.

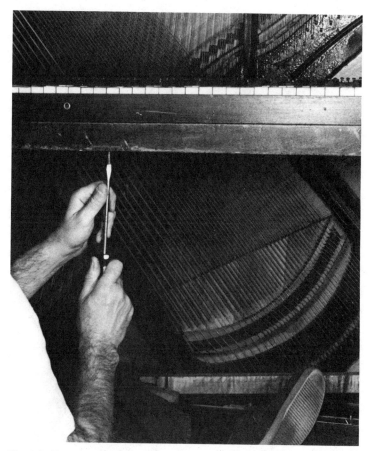

Fig. 4-2. Unscrewing the key slip.

be exposed. Before you start removing the keys, be sure you have a place to store them where they won't get dropped or damaged and where they can be kept in order. This can be a table or a corner of the floor or anywhere that you can put the row of keys down, in order, and leave them for a awhile.

If the tops of the keys are dusty, use your vacuum to clean them. The duster brush attachment works best for cleaning the keys.

All piano keys are numbered. You will see a number stamped into the wooden part of the key about an inch back from the end of the key cover. In Fig. 4-3, the white key at the far left is #1; the black key next to it is #2, followed by #3, etc. Sometimes the numbers are difficult to read. In Fig. 4-3, the numbers from 8 on get increasingly hard to read. If you find it hard to read the numbers

Fig. 4-3. Numbers on the keys.

on your keys, renumber them with a pencil before you remove them. Start with #1 on the lowest key (on your left as you face the piano). It is important for the keys to be replaced in the same order. By numbering the keys, you protect yourself in case they are accidentally dropped or get mixed up somehow.

The best way to remove a key is to grasp it at both ends and lift it straight up (Fig. 4-4). Each key pivots at the center on a pin, called a *balance rail pin*. There is a second pin, the *front rail pin*, under the front edge of each key. Be careful not to bend these pins as you pick up and remove the individual keys.

Small discs made of felt or paper, called *punchings*, will rest over each of these pins. In Fig. 4-4, there are white punchings on the balance rail pins and dark punchings on the front rail pins. When you remove the keys, be sure these punchings stay on the pins so they won't get lost.

Carefully remove the bottom key (#1) and look on the bottom side of it. Many times the person who made the piano keys will have written his name or initial on the bottom of this key. Sometimes the key makers also wrote the date. Put the #1 key on the left side of the table or wherever it will be stored while you are working on the piano. Take out the next key (#2) and place it on the storage table to the right of #1. Continue in this way, keeping the keys in order until all the keys have been removed and placed together on the storage table.

CLEANING THE INSIDE OF THE PIANO

When all the keys have been removed, you will be able to clean the inside of the piano. You might be amazed at the debris you find underneath the keys. Pieces of paper, old playing cards, and coins are common items. One man found a petrified hard-boiled egg inside his piano! If you find any coins in an old piano, you may want to check their dates and consult a book of coin prices. Maybe you will be lucky and find something that's worth far more than its face value. Even if there is nothing that interesting inside your piano, you are certain to find lots of dust and dirt. The vacuum cleaner is the best way to clean the inside of your piano. Use it on normal suction, not reverse, and use the duster brush attachment if you have one. If you don't have a duster brush, you can use the bare nozzle.

A soft paint brush about an inch wide is ideal to use along with the vacuum. With the paint brush, gently whisk the dust and debris toward the nozzle of the vacuum. The paint brush is especially

Fig. 4-4. Removing a piano key.

Fig. 4-5. Using a paint brush to guide dirt into the vacuum.

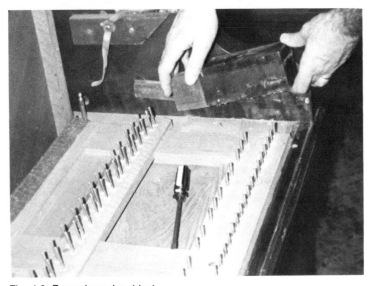

Fig. 4-6. Removing a key block.

52

useful for going around the balance rail pins and the front rail pins (Fig. 4-5). You want to be sure that none of the punchings from these pins go up the vacuum. By using the paint brush, you can get the area around the pins clean without danger of vacuuming up the punchings. The soft bristles of the brush can also get into nooks and crannies that would not be reachable otherwise. It is okay to vacuum the strings, too, with the duster brush attachment. Just be gentle.

REMOVING THE KEY BLOCKS AND KEY FRAME

After you have vacuumed under the keys, remove the two key blocks. Each key block will have a screw that secures it to the key bed. There is usually a pin protruding from the bottom of the key block to keep it in place. After you have removed the screws and marked them, the key block can be lifted straight up off of the securing pins (Fig. 4-6). Be sure to mark the key blocks on the backside Left and Right.

The key frame is the wooden framework that was beneath the keys and has the balance rail pins and the front rail pins sticking up from it. Often there will be at least one large screw sticking up

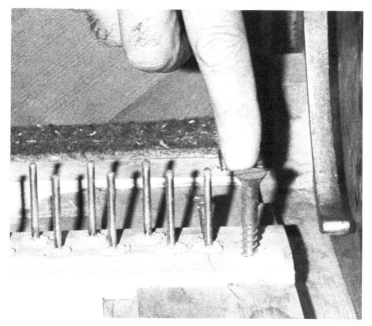

Fig. 4-7. The key cover rests on this screw so it should not be removed.

an inch or so above the key frame at each end. These screws are stops that the key cover rests on and should not be removed (Fig. 4-7). The smaller screws in Fig. 4-7 have been loosened and will be removed before the key frame is lifted off.

At this time you should check the strip of material that runs along the backside of the key frame. This material is called the *back rail cloth*. In Fig. 4-7, the back rail cloth can be seen just at the tops of the balance rail pins. The back rail cloth is about 1 1/2 inches wide and nearly 1/4 inch thick. If it is in good condition, you can just leave it where it is. Sometimes, the back rail cloth has been partially or totally destroyed (usually by moths), and in such a case, it will need to be replaced,. If you need a new back rail cloth, you can order one from one of the piano supply companies found in the suppliers list in the Appendix. Don't attempt to make a back rail cloth using the sort of felt or other fabric that you can purchase at a fabric store. Such materials are not suitable.

Take out all the screws that hold the key frame to the key bed; there will probably be at least a dozen. Sometimes the back rail cloth covers some of the screws. If so, carefully pull the back rail cloth back slightly to remove these screws (Fig. 4-8).

Fig. 4-8. Removing the key frame.

Fig. 4-9. Three wooden spacers that were under the key frame.

Measure each screw as you remove it and write the size and location on your sketch of the key frame. The screws will be in rows running lengthwise. The screws in each row are usually the same size, in which case, you can put them in a paper cup marked "key frame."

When the screws have been removed, gently lift the key frame from the key bed. Fig. 4-8 shows a key frame being removed. Note the good condition of the back rail cloth on this particular piano. As you lift the key frame, look underneath to see if there are any paper or wooden spacers beneath the key frame. If there are, these spacers should be numbered so they can be replaced in the same spots that they came from when you again attach the key frame to the key bed. In Fig. 4-9, the worker is holding three thin wooden spacers that were under the key frame.

After the key frame has been removed, put it where it cannot be tipped over or damaged. You will probably need to vacuum the inside of the piano again now. You can also vacuum the key frame if it needs it.

REMOVING THE LID

The lid should be removed next. On most pianos, only the forward portion of the lid can be taken off; on others, the entire lid is removable. If you can remove the entire lid, do so. If you cannot, then the stationary portion of the lid will have to be stripped in place. If the lid of your piano is hinged, you will need to remove the hinged part. First take out all the screws in the hinge and put them in a paper cup or other container marked "hinge screws from lid." Mark the hinge itself, too, so that it will be returned to its original position. Stick a piece of masking tape on the backside of the hinge and mark it "left end" or "right end." Carefully set this long hinge in a place where it can lie flat. Such hinges are soft, and if you stand them on end, they will bend.

If the hinge is badly rusted or corroded, you may want to replace it. You may be able to buy a replacement hinge locally rather than ordering it by mail. Look in the Yellow Pages of your telephone book under Cabinet Shops or Hinges. You may be able to find someone who sells it by the foot. If not, you can order a new one from one of the piano parts catalogs mentioned earlier.

RUBBER BUMPERS

By now you have probably discovered many places where there are flattened rubber bumpers or where it looks like there used to be rubber bumpers. Many times all that remains is the little nail that once secured the bumper to the piano. These nails look like the brass heads of upholstery tacks. Any of these bumpers or nails that are still on the piano should be gently pried up and removed. Be careful not to damage any of the surrounding wood. A pocket knife works well for prying off these rubber bumpers (Fig. 4-10).

You can throw the old rubber bumpers away because new bumpers are readily available at low cost and will look better than the old ones. Count the old bumpers before you dispose of them so you will know how many new ones to buy. Also, make some notes to yourself so you will remember where they go. After you have stripped and refinished the piano, you can refer to these notes as you put the new rubber bumpers on. Rubber bumpers are also sometimes called *rubber nail heads*, so if you don't find them under one name, try the other.

PROTECTING THE PIANO'S BACK FROM STRIPPER

You should cover the back of your piano to protect it from the stripper. Even though the back of the piano is usually against a wall where it doesn't show, it is such an easy matter to protect it that

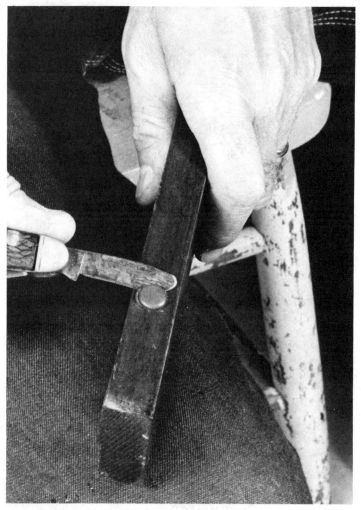

Fig. 4-10. Using a pocket knife to remove a rubber bumper.

you should do so in case you ever want to position the instrument where the back does show.

First, cut some strips of old absorbent cloth about 1 1/2 inches wide. Fold the strips in half lengthwise and staple them across the back side of the piano on the top and sides (Fig. 4-11). If you don't have a staple gun, you can secure the strips of cloth with thumb tacks.

Now, take a sheet of plastic, such as the black plastic which is sold at nurseries, and staple the plastic securely to the cloth. Fig-

Fig. 4-11. Staple pieces of absorbent rag on the back of the piano.

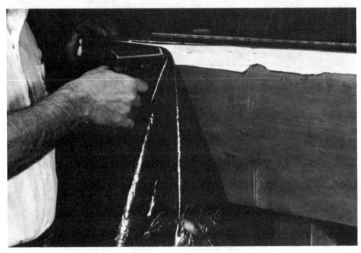

Fig. 4-12. Put plastic over the cloth to protect back from stripper.

ure 4-12 shows the plastic being put on over the strips of absorbent material. Be sure you pull the plastic tight so there aren't any gaps. The plastic will protect the back of your piano, and the cloth will soak up any stripper that manages to run down behind the plastic.

REMOVING THE PEDALS

Often there is a metal plate around the pedals. If your piano has such a plate, remove it.

There will be a threaded rod, approximately long at- 6 inches taching the back of each pedal to the wooden rocker arm. Measure the amount of threaded rod that is exposed above each of the nuts and write this measurement on top of the corresponding rocker arm. You will need these measurements later. Also, note which of the several holes in the pedals the rods are in. In Fig. 4-13, there is 1/2 inch of threaded rod above the rocker arm for the right hand pedal.

When you have these measurements, remove the nut and the

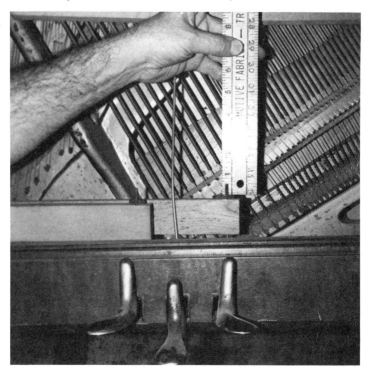

Fig. 4-13. Measure the threaded rod above each rocker arm.

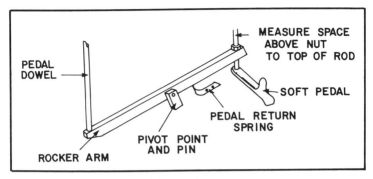

Fig. 4-14. The rocker arm and its attachments.

felt washer from the top of each rod. Also, remove the pivot pin, which is sticking through the side of the rocker arm and allows the rocker arm to rock. The pivot pin can be seen in Fig. 4-14, which shows a rocker arm and all of its attachments. The pivot pin can be pulled out with a pliers.

Next, unscrew the blocks at the back of the pedals. Sometimes these blocks are wood; sometimes they are metal (Fig. 4-15). If the blocks are in more than one piece, mark them "right" and "left."

Fig. 4-15. Unscrewing a block from behind a pedal.

Now you will be able to remove the pedals by pulling them carefully forward through the hole in the bottom rail. There will be pieces of felt on the board surrounding each pedal. You may have to remove these pieces of felt in order to get the pedals out. Pry the felt loose and save the pieces in a cup or envelope. You will want to replace these pieces with new felt, but you will need these old pieces for patterns. Figure 4-16 shows the pedals being removed. The pieces of felt are still in place, and they will be removed next.

PUTTING THE PIANO ON ITS BACK

You are now going to lay the piano on its back. This is necessary in order to remove the piano's legs, and it also makes it much easier to strip the case itself. The piano will be resting on four pieces of 4- × -4, each 8-12 inches long. One 4- × -4 will lie flat under each corner of the piano as shown in Fig. 4-17. Make sure you have ample newspaper or another sheet of plastic spread on the floor on the area where you will be laying the piano down.

For this step of the project you will need some help from at least two of your friends. Three is even better. The piano isn't as heavy now as it was because you have taken so may parts off, but it is still far too heavy and cumbersome to try to lay it down by yourself. Be safe; wait until you have adequate help. When your

Fig. 4-16. Removing the pedals.

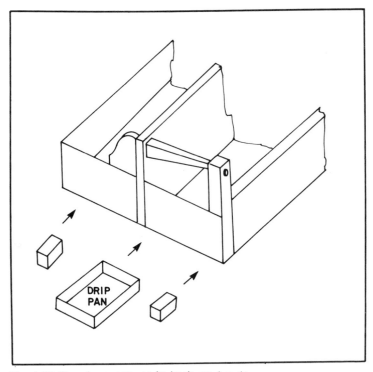

Fig. 4-17. The piano rests, on its back, on 4-×-4s.

friends arrive to help, position two of the 4-×-4s in approximately the place where the top of the piano will be after you have tipped it over.

Two people should stand behind the piano, one on each side. A third person needs to be in front of the piano to keep it from rolling forward. Tip the piano over backward and rest the upper end of it on two of the pieces of 4-×-4. These 4-×-4s will make it easy to put the piano down without pinching your fingers underneath. Now, lift the bottom end of the piano and put the other two 4-×-4s under it. Put all of the 4-×-4s far enough under so that the piano sticks out at least two inches on all sides.

You will be stripping the main case of the piano while it is lying down.

REMOVING THE PIANO LEGS

Most upright pianos have a block of wood that sticks out about 12 inches from the main body of the piano and supports the bottom of the leg. The casters are attached to this block of wood. This piece of wood stays connected to the piano, but the leg above it comes off. Spinet pianos do not have this block of wood as they have free-standing legs.

Look under the block of wood, beneath the bottom of the leg, to see if the screw that goes up into the bottom of the leg is exposed. If it is, remove it. You may have to take off the casters on the front of the piano in order to find the screws that go into the legs. Whether you must remove them or not, this is a good time to check the condition of the casters. If they are broken or split, you will want to order new ones.

After you have removed the screws that go into the bottom of the piano's legs, find the screws that go down through the key bed into the top of the piano legs. These are usually just inside the key cheeks. Remove and measure all screws and record their size and location.

The piano legs should now come off (Fig. 4-18). Note the screw hole just above the caster. This is where the screw went up into the bottom of the piano leg. In this particular piano, there was a smaller block of wood attached to the top of the leg. You can see where the screw holes in the key bed are, which indicate where the screws went down into the top of the piano leg. In order to remove the legs of this piano, it was necessary to take the upper block of wood off as well, as it was attached to the leg with a dowel. This, of course, was desirable, because it is far easier to strip pieces

Fig. 4-18. Removing a piano leg; the piano is on its back.

that have been removed from the case. Not all pianos have a block of wood at the upper end of the piano legs. If yours has one and it will come off, remove it.

If the legs are an especially tight fit, it may be necessary to tap them to the side in order to get them off. If you have a rubber hammer, you can use it. Otherwise, wrap some heavy cloth around a block of wood, hold it against the side of the leg on the inside, and tap the wood with a regular hammer or mallet. Tap alternately at the top and bottom of the leg to work it free without forcing it.

REMOVING THE KEY BED

There may be a screw anchoring the key bed to the metal harp. If so, remove it. You will normally find three large, long screws coming up through the bottom of the key bed on both the left and right sides. These screws anchor the key bed to the bottom of the key cheeks. In Fig. 4-18, two of these screws are visible just under the top of the leg that is being removed. Take these screws out. After you have removed these screws, the key bed should be free. Grasp the key bed and lift it out.

The bottom panel latch is attached to the bottom of the key bed. The action support bolts are attached to the top of the key bed. The bottom panel latch and the action support bolts should not be removed. You will only be stripping the front and edge of the key bed. In Fig. 4-19, you see the action support bolts sticking

Fig. 4-19. Leave the action support bolts on the key bed.

up from the key bed. The bottom panel latch is on the bottom side of the key bed.

REMOVING THE KEY CHEEKS

It is time to remove the two key cheeks. There are usually four large screws holding the key cheeks to the sides of the piano frame. Many times there is also an extra piece of wood attached to the inside of the key cheek. These extra pieces of wood might be covering the screws, which hold the key cheeks to the sides of the piano. Remove any such extra pieces in order to get at the large screws, which hold the key cheeks to the sides of the piano. Mark any such pieces "inside, left key cheek" or "inside, right key cheek."

Because these small extra pieces are not seen from the outside, it won't be necessary to strip them. After you remove them, you can just put the screws back in them until it is time to reattach them to the key cheeks. Be sure to mark and diagram these pieces so you will remember exactly where they go.

After these pieces are off, you can remove the large screws that hold the key cheeks to the sides of the piano. Figure 4-20 shows a key cheek being removed. One of the large screws has been left partly screwed in, so you can see its relative size. Also note the three screw holes where the other screws were.

Sometimes the key cheeks have also been glued to the piano. In this case, you may not be able to remove them. If the key cheeks won't come off after you have removed all the screws, hold a piece of scrap wood against the outside of the key cheek. Using a mallet, give the wood a sharp rap. If the key check doesn't budge, you will have to strip it in place.

DISMANTLING THE REST OF THE PIANO

If there are any more removable pieces, take them off. For example, in a few pianos, the bottom rail that the pedals go through is removable. If so, take it off.

There is one exception to the rule of taking everything apart. Don't remove anything from the key bed, such as the action support bolts. Remember, you only need to strip the front and sides of the key bed.

There may be other pieces of scroll work or gingerbread attached with screws to your piano. Because there are hundreds of styles and manufacturers of pianos, it isn't possible to list here every single possibility. The older pianos, especially, tend to have fancy

Fig. 4-20. Taking off a key cheek.

parts attached to them. If such pieces are on your piano and they can be removed for stripping, remove them.

CAUTION: Do not remove any of the large screws that secure the metal harp to the piano frame. The combined tension of the more

66

than 200 strings attached to the frame exerts more than 18 tons of pressure. Removal of those screws could redistribute the tension and cause the harp to crack. You will not be removing the strings or the harp, so you should not touch any of those screws.

You now have everything major disassembled. Go back and take each individual piece, one at a time, and sketch the location of any hardware that is still attached to it. After sketching, remove the hardware, being sure to mark the screws and their locations so that everything can go back the way it was.

Don't leave any hinges, locks, or other hardware on the piano pieces. Use masking tape to identify individual pieces of hardware.

TAKING APART THE FALLBOARD

The fallboard generally is comprised of three separate pieces of wood, all of which run the full width of the piano. You will need to take these three sections apart in order to strip them.

Piece #1 is the front, curved section that goes over the keys. It will be attached to Piece #2 with a long piano hinge. Remove this hinge, being careful not to bend it, and set it aside. Lay it flat to keep it straight.

Piece #2 is a large piece, which often has a decal of the manufacturer's name on it. It will sit on Piece #3, which was screwed to the key blocks and rests lightly on the keys. Pieces #2 and #3 will probably be connected with three small hinges. Remove these hinges. Figure 4-21 shows the three pieces of a fallboard.

There will be a strip of felt on the bottom of Piece #3. This felt is about 40 inches long and protrudes about 1/16 inch toward the back edge of the black keys. It is visible from the front of the piano when the fallboard is open. This piece of felt is called the *nameboard felt*. Measure the nameboard felt and mark on Piece #3 exactly where the felt goes as it won't run the full width of the piano. You will be removing this nameboard felt, stripping the piece of wood, and then putting on a new piece of felt.

You will need to cut the new piece the same length as the old one and glue it in the same place where the old nameboard felt was, so measure and mark carefully. Add "nameboard felt" to the list of things you plan to order from a piano supply company. The nameboard felt is thicker than the kind of felt sold at fabric stores and meant for ordinary household sewing. Don't try to substitute. There is a new strip of nameboard felt in Fig. 4-21, next to the piece it will be glued to.

Diagram the three pieces of the fallboard. Mark the measure-

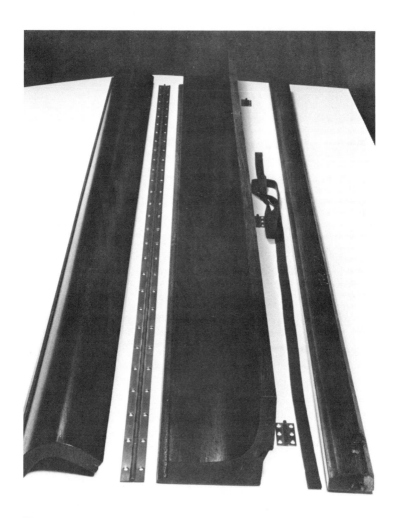

Fig. 4-21. The parts of a fallboard.

ment and location of the nameboard felt as well as size and location of hinges.

If your fallboard has knobs on it, decide if they are worth saving. It is hard to strip such knobs in place, so unless they are especially nice, it will be easier to remove them with pliers and order new knobs. If you decide to get new knobs, put that on your parts list. You should also remove any rubber bumpers that remain on the fallboard, marking the location on your sketch.

Your piano has now been completely taken apart. Everything that will come off, is off. Don't panic! It may look impossible now, but when the time comes, you will be able to put everything back together in the proper order. With no parts left over.

ORDERING THE PARTS YOU NEED

At this time, you should send in your order for whatever parts you are going to replace. Here are some of the parts that you may be ordering:

- ☐ White key covers.
- ☐ Black key covers.
- ☐ Rubber bumpers.
- ☐ Nameboard felt.
- ☐ Fallboard knobs.
- ☐ Back rail cloth.
- ☐ Piece of thick felt for miscellaneous use, such as around the pedals and beneath the rocker arms.
- ☐ Casters.
- ☐ Key.

Key is listed because, if your piano has a keyhole, you may be able to order a key that fits. Most old pianos require a triangular shaped key. You should be able to determine this by looking in the key slot.

Mail your order and payment now. While your order is being filled, you will be busy stripping all of the parts of your piano.

Chapter 5

Stripping Off the Old Finish

Now that your piano is completely taken apart, it is time to strip off the old finish.

STRIPPER INGREDIENTS

If your piano has its original finish (either lacquer, shellac, or varnish), you will be able to mix your own stripping solution at a fraction of the cost of the commercial varieties. If your piano has been painted, you will need to rely on a commercially prepared product, and you won't be mixing your own.

For pianos with an original finish, you will need only two stripper ingredients—denatured alcohol and lacquer thinner. Denatured alcohol is also called shellac thinner, but it is usually more expensive if you buy it that way. Denatured alcohol is the generic name; if you ask for that, it usually costs less.

Both denatured alcohol and lacquer thinner are sold in gallon size containers at most paint or hardware stores. You won't know how much of each you will need until you determine what kind of finish your piano has. Different finishes use different proportions of stripper ingredients. That is why, if you assembled the supplies listed in Chapter 3, you only bought one gallon each to begin with.

DETERMINING WHAT KIND OF FINISH YOUR PIANO HAS

It is easy to learn which kind of finish is on your piano. Open the can of denatured alcohol, put on your rubber gloves, and dip your finger in the denatured alcohol. With your wet finger, vigorously rub a spot on the piano about the size of a 50-cent piece. Keep rubbing for 30 seconds. If the surface of the piano gets gummy and begins to dissolve, you will know the finish is shellac. For pianos with a shellac finish, the denatured alcohol will be the main ingredient that you use in the stripper solution.

If the surface of the piano didn't get gummy and start to dissolve, open the lacquer thinner. Wipe off your finger on a rag or paper towel, dip your finger in the lacquer thinner, and rub a spot on the piano. Rub vigorously for 30 seconds just as you did before. If the finish on the piano begins to dissolve from the lacquer thinner, you will know the finish is lacquer. On pianos with a lacquer finish, the lacquer thinner will be the main ingredient of your stripper. Figure 5-1 shows a piano being tested with lacquer thinner. The dark spot is where the old, cracked finish is getting gummy while the light part, in the center of the circle, is bare wood.

If your piano is varnished, dip your finger in one solvent at a time but keep rubbing for at least a minute. Experiment to see which works best on your kind of varnish, the denatured alcohol or the lacquer thinner. When you know which solvent dissolves your finish best, use it as the main ingredient in your stripper solution.

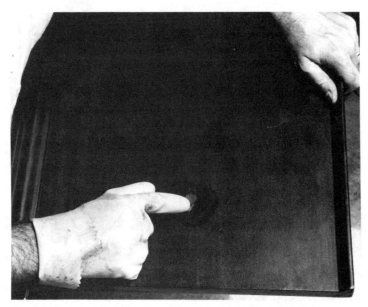

Fig. 5-1. Test spot to determine what kind of finish the piano has.

If your piano was manufactured in the 1950s or 1960s, it may have a varnish on it. This is more difficult to remove than shellac or lacquer, but the denatured alcohol-lacquer thinner mixture will soften most varnishes. You just might have to work at it a little longer.

BUYING THE REST OF THE STRIPPER INGREDIENTS

You will be mixing the solution in a three-to-one ratio. If your piano has a shellac finish, you will need 3 gallons of denatured alcohol and 1 gallon of lacquer thinner. If your piano has a lacquer finish, you will need 3 gallons of lacquer thinner and 1 gallon of denatured alcohol. For a varnished surface, buy three of whichever solvent worked best and one of the other. Table 5-1 gives the correct stripper proportions for various finishes.

You won't need to buy any other ingredients. A total of 4 gallons is plenty for the average upright piano. If you are stripping a grand piano you may need more. Just keep the same three-to-one ratio.

If your piano has been painted, the denatured alcohol-lacquer thinner solution won't work. For a painted piano, you will need to purchase a commercial paint stripper and follow the manufacturer's instructions for its use. A paint store will be able to advise you as to which paint stripper is best for your kind of project.

MIXING THE STRIPPER

To mix the stripper solution, take a 1-gallon can of your main stripping ingredient (lacquer thinner for a lacquer finish; denatured

Table 5-1. Formula Proportions for Stripper.

Shellac Finish
3 gallons denatured alcohol
1 gallon lacquer thinner

Lacquer Finish
3 gallons lacquer thinner
1 gallon denatured alcohol

Varnish Finish
Determine which solvent (lacquer thinner or denatured alcohol) works best to dissolve your kind of varnish. Use three parts of it, to one part of the other.

Painted Finish
Buy paint stripper and follow directions

---

alcohol for a shellac finish) and pour off 1 quart into a different container. A 2-pound coffee can works fine. Be sure to label the can so you will remember what is in it and cover it tightly so the liquid won't evaporate. Now fill the gallon can of solvent back up with your second ingredient. This will give you the proper three-to-one ratio that you need.

Example: If your piano has a shellac finish, your main ingredient will be denatured alcohol. Take a gallon of denatured alcohol and pour 1 quart of it into another container. Then pour lacquer thinner into the gallon can of denatured alcohol until it is full again. Cover the can and shake to mix.

STRIPPING SUPPLIES

For the stripping process, you will need the large pan listed earlier. You will be putting one end of the piece you are stripping into this pan as you work. This allows you to use the stripper generously as it will run down the piece and into the pan. You can then reuse it. The pan also saves a good deal of splattering on the floor.

You will also need your rubber gloves, a supply of 0000 (extra fine) steel wool, and a multi-purpose cleaning pad. It helps to have an old box or low stool to sit on as you work.

Spread a generous amount of newspaper in the area where you will be working to catch any accidental splashes. Your stripping should always be done in a well ventilated place. If you are using a garage, be sure the doors are open while you are working with the stripper, and stay far away from the pilot light on either a furnace or hot water heater. There should be no smoking allowed near the area where you are stripping. Good ventilation also minimizes the smell of the fumes. In nice weather, the stripping can be done out of doors, but it is best to stay in the shade because direct sunlight will make the solvents evaporate too quickly.

HOW TO USE THE STRIPPER

Put on your rubber gloves before you begin. Even if you have tough skin that isn't bothered by solvents, you will want to wear rubber gloves because the stripper is soon going to be a sticky mess, and it will be much easier to remove a pair of gloves then to clean the mucky dark finish from your hands and fingernails.

A useful trick when stripping is to roll the top edge of your rubber gloves down about an inch to form a cuff. When your hands are held upward as you work, the stripper wants to run down the gloves and right on down your arms. By forming a cuff on each glove, the cuff will catch any drippings. Ocassionally, you can tip your hands down and allow the accumulation to run out into the pan.

Begin with a small, straight piece of wood, such as one of the key cheeks rather than one that has carving or grooves. You need to get the hang of it first before you start the fancy stuff.

If you are using steel wool, tear a ball in half and use only one half at a time. Half a piece will last almost as long as a whole piece, will work just as well, and will let you get alot more mileage from your steel wool supply. Eventually the steel wool will get clogged with old finish and will need to be replaced.

If you are using one of the green pads, use the whole thing. On large pieces, the all-purpose pads work better than steel wool. The loosened finish doesn't accumulate and get clogged in them the way it does with steel wool. They are usually more economical than steel wool, too. The following directions will use the word "pad," meaning either the all-purpose cleaning pad or a pad of steel wool, whichever you are using.

Pour some of your stripping solution into an empty coffee can. Fill the can about one-third full. Set the coffee can in your large pan. Put one end of the piece you are going to strip first into the pan. Now dip your pad into the stripping solution and saturate it thoroughly. Use the pad to saturate the piano piece with stripper. At this time, don't scrub with the pad, just use it to slosh the stripper on the wood. Be generous because it is going to run back into the pan and not be wasted. It isn't just the scrubbing action that removes the old finish, it is the softening action of the solvents. They should do most of the work, not you. Your job is merely to remove the softened surface.

For the first minute or two, concentrate on keeping the piece well saturated. You will save lots of energy if you don't start scrubbing until the finish is soft. When the finish starts to get soft and gummy, scrub the board lightly with the pad working an area 1 or 2 feet square at a time and always rubbing with the grain of the wood.

When you first start stripping a piece, it may be difficult to tell which way the grain of the wood is running. Grain will always run lengthways on long pieces. Don't worry if you cannot tell right away; until you actually reach the wood, you cannot make any marks on it through the finish anyway. When you do reach the wood, you will be able to see which way the grain is going. In Fig.

5-2, one end of a music shelf has been worked with stripper. It is easy to see which way the grain of the wood runs once the old finish starts to come off.

Sometimes it is necessary to make a few light strokes against the grain in order to remove the finish. Just don't get violent in these across-the-grain movements or you will end up with permanent swirls on your finished piano.

If the piece needs to be stripped on more than one side, work all surfaces at the same time. Apply the stripper to all sides and then keep turning the piece, rubbing with the pad on one side at a time. This way, while you are working one side with the pad, the other sides are being softened.

Saturate the pad with stripper frequently. Dip the pad into the solution in the bottom of the pan and then squeeze the pad to keep

Fig. 5-2. Stripping a music shelf.

Fig. 5-3. Rest one end of long pieces on a ladder while stripping the other end.

the old, softened finish removed from the pad.

When you are stripping large pieces, work the bottom foot or two until all the finish seems to be off. Then, move up the piece the next couple of feet. If it is quite a long piece, turn it over when you get to the middle and put the other end in the pan. It will help when you are stripping long pieces, such as the lid or fallboard, to rest the top of the piece on a step ladder to help support it while you work on the bottom half. In Fig. 5-3, one end of the music shelf is resting on the ladder while the other end gets stripped.

The key to proper stripping is patience. Don't try to rush it.

If you do only one or two pieces of the piano in an evening, you are doing fine, and they will soon add up. At the end of a week, you will find the whole piano has been stripped. If you hurry, you won't give the solvents enough chance to work for you, so take your time. Listen to the ball game or some music while you work. This should be a labor of love, not a hard, strenuous task to be finished at breakneck speed. Let the solvents work and you won't have to.

SAVING USED STRIPPER FOR REUSE

Eventually, as the solvent removes the finish, the mixture in the pan will get thick and syrupy. When this happens, pour it into an empty can and cover and label the can. Coffee cans or shortening cans work well. Let the can sit overnight so the heavy solids will settle to the bottom. When you begin work the next time, you can pour the thinner solution off the top of the can into your drip pan and use it again. The muck that settles to the bottom gets discarded. By doing this, you don't waste any of the solvent.

You will probably fill a 2-pound coffee can with syrupy mixture for every two or three hours that you strip.

STRIPPING GROOVES AND CARVINGS

When you start stripping the turned legs or any pieces that have carving or grooves, you may need more than just the pad in order to remove all of the softened finish from the grooves. A small, stiff brush can be used. Old toothbrushes are fine. Be sure to keep the piece thoroughly moistened with stripper so the old finish will soften and be easier to remove. Don't ever use sharp tools, such as screwdrivers or knives, to remove stripper. It is too easy to slip and permanently damage the wood.

Wooden Popsicle sticks can be sharpened slightly on one end to make a point and will work well for removing the finish from grooves and crevices. Such a stick is being used in Fig. 5-4 to help get the softened finish out from the bottom of the music shelf. These sticks let you gouge out the softened material without taking a chance of permanently harming the surface if your hand should slip.

The small, round pointed sticks, which cooks use to make mock drumsticks, are another possibility, especially for very small areas. Pieces of old wooden clothespins make excellent tools because they are made of hard wood and retain a point well.

If there are some deep grooves going around your piano legs, get a piece of coarse twine or heavy string. After the stripper has

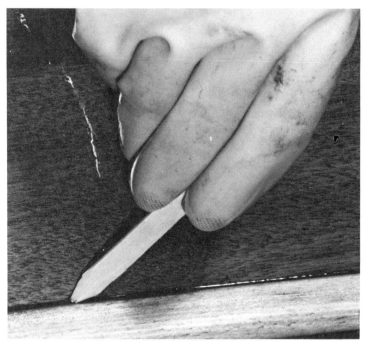

Fig. 5-4. Using a wooden stick to remove softened finish from a crevice.

softened the finish on the legs, saw the twine back and forth in the grooves (Fig. 5-5). It will remove the softened finish nicely. Go slowly for best results.

APPLYING FRESH STRIPPER

When you think you have all the old finish off a piece, set it aside to dry. At the end of your day's work, pour the used stripper into the can to let it settle, as above, for reuse. Then put fresh stripper in your pan and take a fresh pad. Go over each piece a second time with this clean stripper and pad, saturating each board completely one more time.

Quickly take an absorbent rag (old bath towels are perfect) and wipe all the solution from the surface of the wood. By doing this, any shellac or lacquer that is dissolved in the stripping solution does not reapply itself to the wood as the mixture evaporates.

If desired, you can wait until you have stripped the entire piano and then go back over each piece with fresh stripper and a fresh pad, wiping off the solution on a rag as quickly as possible.

LET STRIPPED PIECES DRY

After you have gone over a piece the second time, allow it to dry for at least two hours. By then, it will be easy to see if there are any spots that have not been completely stripped. Look at each piece from different angles in good light to be sure you haven't

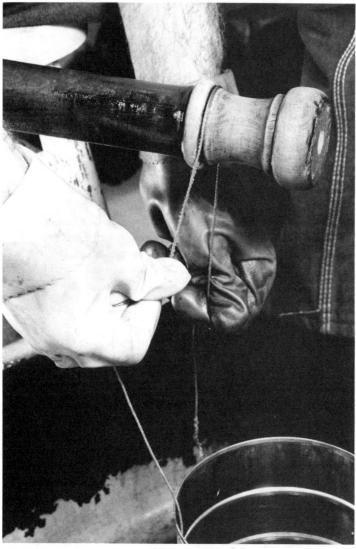

Fig. 5-5. Coarse twine will get softened finish out of grooves on the piano legs.

missed any places. Any shellac or lacquer that has not been removed from the piano will look shiny and be quite noticeable.

If there are any such spots, use fresh stripper and a clean pad to go back over the piece one more time. Rub the area thoroughly to be sure the spot has been removed, and then quickly use a clean rag to wipe the entire piece. You have to be sure that the material you soften does not redeposit itself elsewhere on the piece, so go over the entire piece with solvent before you dry it.

Now let the piece dry another 2 hours or more.

PROTECTING THE HARP

Before you start to strip the main portion of the piano, you will need to cover the harp. You don't want to get any of the stripping solution on the harp, strings, or sounding board.

The easiest way to protect the harp is with more rags and another sheet of plastic, the same way you covered the back of the piano. Staple or tack the rags and plastic so that any spillage or drips will fall on the face of the plastic. There is usually enough space across the top and along the sides of the harp to attach such protection. Don't staple the rags and plastic to the sounding board; staple them to the sides of the piano frame. For extra protection, put a rag inside the piano, on top of the plastic, adjacent to the area you are working on. The rag will help to catch drips, and it is easy to move the rag as you work a new area.

STRIPPING THE CASE

You will be stripping the sides and top of the piano while it is still on its back. Because it is probably not high enough off the floor for your large pan to fit underneath, you will need to use a paint roller pan for this portion of your work.

Slide the pan under the piano and then strip one small section at a time, being careful always to work with the grain of the wood. As you finish one section, move your rag and your roller pan and begin the next section. Continue in this way until you have stripped both sides and the top of the piano. Then pour your solution into the can for reuse. Take fresh stripper and a clean pad and go back over one whole side, working as quickly as possible, and immediately wiping it down with a clean absorbent rag. Do the same for the top and the other side.

When the whole case has been gone over with the fresh stripper and wiped down, let it dry for at least 2 hours. Then examine it carefully to be sure all the old finish has been removed. If you still see traces of old finish, go over the entire side again with clean stripper. Don't try to strip only a small spot, or you will end up with lines showing where you worked. Instead, go quickly back over the entire piece one more time. Be fussy. You don't want the finished product to be marred by small spots you missed.

WATER MARKS AND CIGARETTE BURNS

The lacquer thinner/denatured alcohol formula is especially good for removing the white-colored water marks that are often found in rings, where wet glasses were left on the wood. Such water marks should come off with the stripping solution without doing anything else to the wood.

Another common disfiguration in old pianos is cigarette burns. These are usually found on the key blocks and occasionally on the lid. When stripping these, use steel wool to rub away as much of the burn as possible. If the burns are very deep, it sometimes isn't possible to remove the entire burn.

Because the key blocks are usually veneer, you can replace the veneer if you have cigarette burns that are too deep. Instructions for replacing veneer are in Chapter 6.

STORING YOUR SUPPLIES

At the end of each day's work, wash your rubber gloves off in the solvent and lay them aside to dry. You may find that you splashed some of the solvent on your arms. If so, take a piece of rag, dip it into fresh stripper, and wipe the spots from your skin before you wash.

Flatten solvent-soaked rags on a concrete floor to dry or soak them in water to avoid spontaneous combustion.

BUFFING THE STRIPPED PIANO

When every part has been completely stripped and allowed to dry and you can no longer see any traces of the old finish, you can proceed to the buffing process.

In order to assure a hard, satin-like finish, you must buff each piece with clean, dry 0000 steel wool. This will remove any faint traces of the original finish that may have been redeposited on the wood. It will also assure you of a smooth, even finish before you start the staining and final finishing process.

When you are doing this buffing, wear lightweight cotton gloves—the kind meant for gardening. In order to get the amount of friction you need, you must apply some pressure, and if you don't have gloves on, you may get blisters on your fingers or palms. Also, the steel wool is hard on your fingertips.

The buffing should always be done in the direction of the grain of the wood, just as the stripping was. Buffing the pieces with steel wool will bring down the grain of the wood, which was slightly raised by the stripper. If your piano was painted and you used paint stripper, you will probably need to do more buffing than if you were able to use the lacquer thinner/denatured alcohol solution.

When you finish buffing each piece, use the duster brush of your vacuum and a soft, cotton rag, such as an old T-shirt, to remove the surface dust and the tiny pieces of steel wool, which are left behind. When each piece is done, it should feel smooth and even to your bare hands.

Continue buffing until you have done the entire piano.

Keys, Pedals, and
Other Special Problems

Each piano has different flaws, which need to be corrected. This chapter discusses some of the most common problems and how to solve them.

REPLACING THE WHITE KEY COVERS

If the white keys on your piano are chipped, cracked, missing, or badly yellowed, you will probably want to replace them. Mail order sources for new key covers are listed in the Appendix.

When you took the piano apart, you were careful to keep the keys in numerical order. As you replace the covers, continue to keep the keys in the right order.

Soften the Old Glue

In order to remove the old key covers, you need to soften the glue that attaches the key covers to the wooden keys. This can be done with the help of a clothes iron. Old irons can be purchased for very little at second hand stores or garage sales. You don't need a steam iron. It is possible, of course, to use your good iron, but you take the chance of getting plastic or glue on the bottom of it.

Set the heat range on the iron for WOOL or at the lower end of the COTTON setting. When it is hot, put it on top of the white key covers on the bottom four or five keys. After about 30 seconds, lift up the iron and see if the key cover is loosened. It is important

Fig. 6-1. Soften the old glue with an iron.

to get the key warm enough so that the cover will peel off easily; otherwise, you risk pulling up some of the wooden key along with the cover. Use a higher heat setting if necessary. Figure 6-1 shows some old white key covers being softened with an iron.

Remove the Old Covers

When the key covers and glue are soft, remove the cover from the first key. Use your pocket knife or a screwdriver to pry the key cover off, and peel the old white key cover off the key (Fig. 6-2).

Meanwhile, put the iron back on the keys, moving it up to include one new key. When you have finished prying off the first key cover, move the iron up another notch and let it stay on the keys while you take the cover off the second key. Continue until all the old white key covers are off. If you should accidentally split one of the wooden keys while you are removing the key cover, carefully pry the split piece of wood off the key cover and glue it back in place. Use a good wood glue for this rather than white glue, which is intended for paper products. After you glue the two parts together, put a heavy rubber band around the key to hold the pieces in place until they are dry.

When all the key covers are off, lightly sand the tops of the wooden keys to make a smooth surface.

Clean the Sides of the Keys

The sides of the wooden keys, at the top front edge, probably look dirty. Usually there is a diagonal line, about 1/4 to 1/2 inch deep, where oil and dirt from the pianist's fingers have soiled the sides of the keys. If you refer back to Fig. 6-2, this soiled line is clearly visible on the side of the key.

Clean the sides of the keys be buffing them with fine steel wool (Fig. 6-3). It will take only a minute or so to do each key, and it will make the keys look like new. When you press down the keys to play your piano, it is nice to have the wooden part that shows look fresh and clean instead of soiled.

Put the New Key Covers on

Use a good grade contact cement to glue the new white key covers on to the wooden keys. Most other glues will soften or spot the key covers if you should accidentally get any on top of them.

Put the contact cement on the back of the new key cover and on the top of the wooden key. Allow them to dry before the parts are put together. Read the manufacturer's instructions carefully for whatever contact cement you use. Most of the instructions will caution you that once the two pieces are joined, the bond is instant. After it has made contact with the key, you cannot slide the key cover around in order to line it up straight. Any excess contact ce-

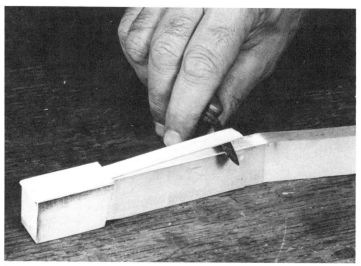

Fig. 6-2. Prying off the old key cover.

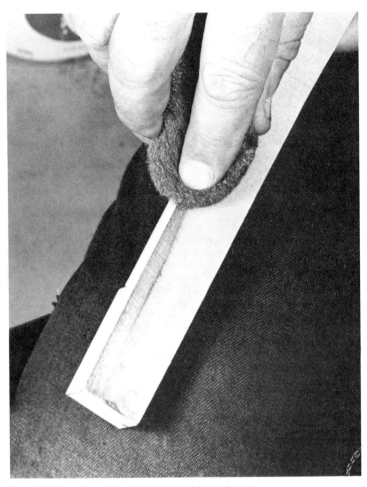

Fig. 6-3. Clean the sides of the keys with steel wool.

ment can usually by removed with lacquer thinner. Again, check the glue container for instructions.

If you put the narrow end of the key cover on the key and hold it down while you lay the rest of the key cover on, it should go on straight and not need adjusting (Fig. 6-4).

File off Excess Cover

Sometimes the back edge of the new white key cover is longer than the back edge of the wooden key at the wide part of the cover. The back edge of the cover should not extend beyond the wood.

Fig. 6-4. Putting on a new white key cover.

Figure 6-5 shows a white key cover that is too big; the excess cover is the part indicated by the dotted line. If your new key covers are too big at that place, use a file to file off the excess cover so that the cover is flush with the wood (Fig. 6-6).

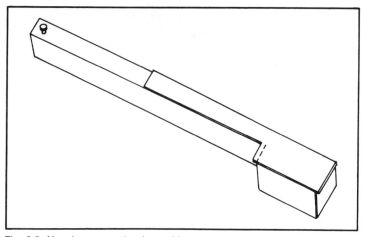

Fig. 6-5. New key cover that is too big.

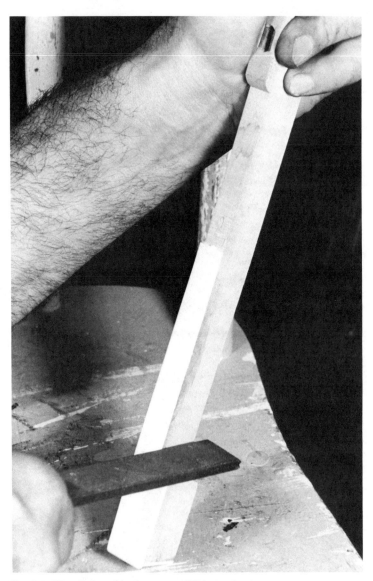

Fig. 6-6. File off the white key cover if it is too long.

Sometimes the new white key covers are slightly wider than the old covers. If this seems to be the case, don't try to correct it at this time. It may not make any difference. When you put the keys back on the piano, you will discover if the extra width causes a problem. If it does, you can correct it at that time.

REPLACING THE BLACK KEY COVERS

Usually it isn't necessary to replace the key covers on the black keys. They are seldom as badly worn as the white key covers are. If they are badly chipped, however, you may want to replace them.

Follow the same directions for replacing the black key covers as the white key covers. Use an iron to soften the glue. If may take more heat to penetrate the wood and loosen the covers on the black keys than it took for the white ones.

Sometimes it is necessary to use a wood chisel and mallet in order to remove the black key covers after they have been heated. A sharp rap of the wood chisel against the back end of the black key cover at the point where the key cover is glued to the wooden key will separate the two nicely (Fig. 6-7).

Use contact cement to attach the new black key covers to the keys.

Painting the Old Black Key Covers

Worn looking black keys can often be rejuvenated with a coat of black lacquer spray paint. If you are going to paint the black key covers, it is not necessary to remove them from the wooden keys. Unless the black keys are badly chipped, paint is the easiest way to make them look fresh and new.

Spread newspaper on a table, and then line up all the black keys, keeping them in order. Buff each black key with steel wool to remove any traces of oil or dirt. If you don't do this, the natural oil from fingers that is on the black keys will prevent the paint from sticking properly. Leave enough space between the keys so that you can paint the side of the keys as easily as the tops.

Automotive supply stores often sell black lacquer spray paint. Be sure to buy a good quality paint so that it will last. Follow directions on the can and spray all the black parts of the keys thoroughly. Let them dry completely before moving them.

CLEANING THE ORIGINAL KEY COVERS

If the original key covers on your piano are not missing or badly chipped, there is no need to replace them. If they are yellow and dirty looking, there are ways to clean them and make them look better.

First try some denatured alcohol. Pour a little on a soft cloth and clean the keys with it. If that does not help, try gently rubbing the keys with 0000 steel wool. Do not press too hard. Often a gen-

Fig. 6-7. Use a wood chisel and mallet to remove a black key cover.

tle buffing with fine steel wool will remove the yellow without damaging the ivory. Yogurt can also be used to clean the keys. Just rub a little yogurt on with a soft cloth.

You should also clean the sides of the wooden keys with steel wool. Complete directions are given earlier in this chapter under the section. "Clean the Sides of the Keys."

THE PEDALS

The pedals are another part of the piano that may require some

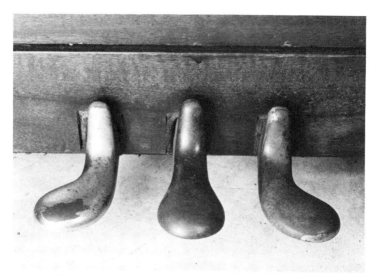

Fig. 6-8. A set of pedals as they were.

special attention. It is possible to order new pedals, but unless your pedals are broken, this should not be necessary. It is not difficult to make the old pedals look good. Figure 6-8 is a set of pedals as they looked before they were removed from the piano.

First, try buffing the pedals with 0000 steel wool. This simple step often removes all the rust and dirt and leaves the pedals looking shiny and new.

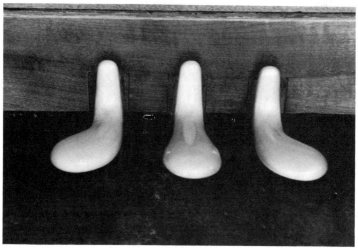

Fig. 6-9. The same pedals after being painted.

If the pedals don't clean up enough with the plain steel wool, try mixing 3 tablespoons of lemon juice with 1 teaspoon of salt. When the salt is dissolved, dip your steel wool into the mixture and rub the pedal with it. Wet the whole pedal with lemon/salt mixture and then let it stand for an hour. Rinse the pedal with clear water and dry it. Repeat this procedure if necessary. Then buff the pedal with dry steel wool to shine it.

If the pedals still don't look good, you can spray paint them with gold or silver paint (Fig. 6-9). Buy a good quality paint. Wipe the pedals with a clean rag to be sure they are free of dust before you paint them. Let the paint dry thoroughly. Then, apply two coats of urethane, letting the pedals dry well in between coats.

Another option is to take the pedals to be replated. Most large cities have companies who do plating. Check the Yellow Pages.

REPLACING CHIPPED VENEER

Sometimes a piano will have a large chip where a piece of wood is actually missing. Such chips are usually at the bottom edge of the side of the piano. You can minimize such badly chipped places

Fig. 6-10. Cut a straight line around the edges of chipped veneer.

Fig. 6-11. Remove all jagged veneer within the straight lines.

by covering them with a new piece of veneer.

Using a single edge razor blade, carefully cut a line around the edges of the chip. Use a ruler or some other straight edge for a guide so that the missing piece will have a straight line around it on all sides. In Fig. 6-10, the line across the top of the chipped veneer is being cut with an X-Acto knife. Straight lines have already been cut down both sides of the chipped area.

Next, use your single edge razor blade, an X-Acto knife, or a small, sharp wood chisel to remove all the jagged pieces of veneer within your straight line. In Fig. 6-11, an X-Acto knife is being used to peel away the ragged veneer. You want to create a square or rectangular space to be repaired, rather than the uneven edges of the original chip.

Sometimes it is more than just the veneer that has been damaged. Especially along the bottom edges of the piano, it is not uncommon to find a fairly deep gouge. In such cases, you need to fill in the hole with wood filler.

Use a small spatula to smooth out the wood filler, making it as even across the surface as possible. Don't bring the wood filler

Fig. 6-12. Fill holes with wood filler.

up flush with the sides of the piano, however. You still have to put
the new veneer on top of the wood filler, so leave enough room
for it. Figure 6-12 shows wood filler being used to fill a hole in the
piano under where the chipped veneer was removed.

You will need to buy a piece of veneer to match the kind of
wood that your piano is made of. If your piano is walnut, buy a
piece of walnut veneer; if your piano is oak, buy oak veneer. Veneer can be found at most lumber stores, many hardware stores,
and any specialty woodworking shops. If you cannot match the color
of the veneer to your stripped wood exactly, don't worry. The finish
that you put on the piano will help to make slightly different shades
of wood look much more alike. Even if it doesn't match perfectly,
it will look far better than the big chip looked.

After you have your new piece of veneer, carefully measure
the size of the hole that you will be covering. Then, cut a new piece
of veneer to fit (Fig.6-13). Make sure the grain of the wood on the
veneer is going in the same direction as the grain of the wood on
the piano. Use contact cement to put the new piece of veneer in
place. Line up the shortest edge of the piece and carefully lay the
veneer in place (Fig. 6-14).

Figure 6-15 shows a close-up of the patched veneer. The

94

outlines of the patch are still visible, but it is a big improvement over the big chip of missing wood.

Refer back to Fig. 6-10, where the straight lines are being drawn around the chip. Notice how apparent the chip is. Figure 6-16 is the same piano, from the same distance, after the veneer was patched. The chip is barely noticeable.

PUTTING NEW VENEER ON KEY BLOCKS

You can also use veneer to cover the key blocks if they are too badly damaged to look good after they are stripped. Usually cigarette burns are the big culprits when it comes to damaged key blocks.

If you plan to put new veneer on your key blocks, you first need to remove the old veneer. Use an old iron, set it at medium heat. Rest it on the key block until the heat from the iron softens the glue that is holding the veneer in place. If you replaced the key

Fig. 6-13. Cut a new piece of veneer.

Fig. 6-14. Put the new veneer in place.

covers on your piano, you are already familiar with the iron technique.

Leave the iron on the key block until the glue is soft enough that the old veneer will peel off. Put the iron on for a few seconds

Fig. 6-15. Patched veneer, close-up.

Fig. 6-16. Patched veneer from normal distance.

and then test the veneer. If it does not come up easily, put the iron on for a few seconds more. Keep checking every 5 to 6 seconds until the veneer comes off easily.

Measure the old piece of veneer, and cut the new piece slightly larger. Use contact cement to glue the new veneer on to the key block. When the glue is completely dry, use a file to gently remove any excess veneer until you get a perfect fit.

Even if only one key block is badly damaged, you will probably want to put new veneer on both of them so that both sides of the piano look the same.

USING NEW DECORATIVE PIECES TO COVER FLAWS

If there is a big gouge or chip on the top of your piano, you may want to camouflage it rather than patching it with new veneer. The patching technique works well for the bottom edges of the piano, where the patch is some distance from the eye. The top of a piano comes in for much closer scrutiny and even the finest patched veneer will still be noticeable. Depending on the style of your piano, there are several ways to cover noticeable flaws.

One way is to buy some unfinished pieces of wooden scrollwork. These pieces come in various shapes and sizes, including fancy scrolls, eagles, and plain geometrical shapes. They also come in a variety of woods. You can buy such pieces at lumber stores, hardware stores, and hobby shops.

These unfinished pieces can be attached to the surface of the piano, over the gouged area, with small, fancy nails. The trick is to make the attachments look like they belong—first by choosing a piece that is consistent with the piano's style and second by using more than one piece.

For example, if the piano has a big gouge in the top on the left end, you might cover the gouge with a piece of scrollwork. Then you would also put a matching scroll in the same place on the right end of the piano.

If the top corners of the piano are badly damaged, you can buy brass corner plates that will cover them. Again, be sure to make the whole piano match.

Figure 6-17 shows a piano with a badly chipped top corner and a deep gouge on the top of the lid. (Remember the piano with the bullet holes that was mentioned in Chapter 1? That is the piano

Fig. 6-17. Piano lid with chipped corner and gouge on top.

Fig. 6-18. The same piano with a brass corner plate and a decorative scroll.

shown in Fig. 6-17. Two of the bullet holes are visible.) Figure 6-18 is the same piano with a piece of scrollwork covering the gouge and a brass corner plate hiding the damaged corner. Figure 6-19 is the other end of the piano; note that it also has brass corner plates and a matching piece of scrollwork.

Fig. 6-19. The other end of the piano with matching scroll and corner plates.

You should wait until you have applied your oil stain before you buy any of these decorative cover-up pieces. Sometimes the flaws are not nearly as obvious after the piano has been stained, and you may decide just to leave it the way it is.

If you do buy some scrollwork or other decorative pieces, they should be stained and finished separately and then attached to the piano. It may be necessary to use more stain on such unfinished pieces than you need on the piano itself in order to get them the same color.

Naturally, you would not attach any brass corner plates until the piano has been completely refinished.

The ways you can use extra, decorative pieces to enhance the beauty of your piano are limited only by your own imagination. Before the piano on the cover of this book was refinished, the front

Fig. 6-20. A lion's head ring instead of a knob on a front panel.

panel had two broken knobs that were meant to be used to pull the front panel forward to form a music rack. Instead of replacing the broken knobs with similar knobs, the owner chose to buy two brass lion's head rings (Fig. 6-20). The lion's head rings are functional and add a unique touch to the front of the piano. They are also in keeping with the overall classic style of this particular piano. So use your imagination when you are deciding how to make your piano special.

CLEAN ALL HARDWARE

The last step in the stripping process is to clean any hardware that you took off the piano. You will want to clean all the hinges, such as the long hinge from the fallboard and the hinge from the lid. Use a new, dry all-purpose pad to clean and buff these hinges. This will remove any rust and oxidized film. Then spray the hinges with WD-40 and shine them with a soft, clean rag. The WD-40 will keep the metal from corroding so fast and also lubricates the hinges.

Do the same thing with the rest of the hardware, such as small hinges. If your piano has a lock, use this same method to clean and shine the keyhole. Making all of the hardware look clean and shiny will add a great deal to the beauty of your refinished piano.

Chapter 7

Applying the New Finish

The hardest part of your project is over, and now you get the fun of putting a lovely new finish on your piano.

YOUR FAVORITE FINISH

If you are experienced at furniture refinishing, you may already have a favorite method and a certain kind of finish that you prefer to use. If so, go ahead and use it. Except for being bigger and more complicated, a piano is like any other fine piece of furniture, and you can put the same finish on it that you would put on a table or hutch. The only difference is that you will be finishing individual pieces of wood and then assembling them later. If you already know how you want your piano finished, do it that way and then proceed to Chapter 8.

TWO EASY FINISHES

If you have never done any kind of furniture refinishing before, you will want to use a finish that is uncomplicated and easy to do well. Of course, you want a beautiful look, too. Following are instructions for two easy ways to finish a piano. Both of them are simple to do, look good, and will give a fine quality finish.

Oil Finish

An oil finish is the easiest finish—both to apply and to maintain. It is an attractive, soft-looking finish that allows all of the patina of the wood to show.

With an oil finish, it isn't necessary to stain the wood first. There are oil stains available that combine these two steps of the usual refinishing process into one step. Even if you want to darken the color of your wood, you don't need to apply a separate coat of stain.

Maintenance of an oil finish is simple, too. It consists of an occasional light reapplication of the oil. In future years, if the finish of the piano should get scratched or marred, it is easily touched up with fresh oil.

You will need to decide what color you want your piano to be. Oil finishes come in a variety of shades ranging from a clear, natural oil, which will bring out the natural grain and color of the wood, to dark shades, such as walnut or mahogany.

You would be wise to test more than one oil stain to see which you like best on your particular wood. Use the back side of the top panel or some other inside piece that won't show. Rub a small amount of the different oil stains into the wood and see which shade you like best. Often, the paint stores that sell these products will do a test patch for you before you buy the oil stain. Take a piece of your wood in to the store. You should go at a time when the store is least busy so the clerk will be able to spend some time with you.

A piano that has been stripped with the lacquer thinner/denatured alcohol solution will usually not absorb as much stain as you think it is going to, so you will want to test a spot before you purchase enough for the entire piano.

Most older pianos are made of more than one kind of wood. Often the main body of the piano will be a hard wood such as oak, but the turned legs and any carved, decorative pieces may be a soft wood, such as pine. Naturally, these different woods will look different when you put the oil stain on them.

Many people like the different shades of wood color that result when the same stain is used on more than one kind of wood. If you prefer to have all the pieces look the same, however, you will need to experiment on your particular piano pieces and use oil stains of varying shades in order to achieve the overall sameness you desire.

If you have used any new veneer, either to patch a hole or on the key blocks, you will find that it may require less stain than the old wood does in order to get the same color.

It will take about a quart of oil to finish an upright piano. When you are ready to apply an oil finish, spread all of the individual piano pieces out, putting them on blocks of wood, sawhorses, inverted corrugated boxes, or whatever else is handy to get them up off the floor. Be sure to spread newspaper underneath them to catch any drips.

It is okay to work outside but keep the pieces out of the direct sunlight. The oil will dry too quickly in the sun. Also, be sure to work where there isn't any dust blowing around.

Wear your rubber gloves while you are applying the oil stain. Otherwise, the oil will get under your fingernails and leave a stain that takes days to get out.

Shake the can of oil finish well and pour some into a container about the size of a 1-pound cottage cheese carton. Cut a piece of rag about 4 inches square—an old towel or wash cloth works well. Saturate the rag with oil stain and apply a liberal coat to all surfaces that will show. After every piece has been coated with the oil stain, wait 15 minutes, and then, using the same rag, spread the oil around again. It won't be necessary to add more oil unless an area is already dry. Wait another 15 minutes. Then go back over every piece and apply a light coat of more oil. You won't need as much this time because it won't soak into the wood like it did the first time. Wait another half an hour, and then, take a soft, dry cloth and wipe each piece to remove all the excess oil. Let the pieces dry overnight.

The next day, use a soft, clean rag to give each piece a dry rub down. This will remove any traces of oil that have worked up from cracks or joints. If there are any traces of oil that have worked up from the wood grain and dried too dark, wipe a rag soaked in fresh oil over the area. This will redissolve the dried oil. Wipe the whole piece again with a dry cloth. Hold each piece in a good light and check to see that no spots have been missed.

Sometimes a small nick in the piano frame will not stain as dark as the surrounding wood. an easy way to cover such minor flaws is with a felt-tip marking pen. After the oil finish has dried completely, use a black or brown felt-tip pen, or even a little of each, to cover the nick and blend it in with the color of the surrounding wood.

If you like the soft, flat finish that the pieces now have, you can proceed to Chapter 8. A piano with this kind of oil finish is easy to care for. It needs no waxing. All it will need is an occasional light coat of oil, which will go on quickly and easily.

Urethane Finish

If you prefer a finish that is a bit more hard and shiny than the plain oil finish, you can achieve this by putting urethane on over the oil finish. Apply the oil finish exactly as directed above. Allow it to dry completely, for at least 24 hours, and then apply two coats of urethane to the pieces.

Buy a good quality urethane. Thin it out slightly with whatever is recommended on the can for thinning. For example,

Fig. 7-1. A piece of coat hanger helps remove excess urethane from the paint brush.

Varathane brand urethane suggests thinning with mineral spirits. If you use Varathane brand on your piano, mix 4 parts Varathane with 1 part mineral spirits. The four-to-one ratio works well with other brands, too. Thinning the urethane helps to keep bubbles out of the liquid and makes it easier to apply a smooth, even coat.

Use a soft, clean brush to apply the urethane finish. A useful trick when working with urethane is to attach a piece of thick wire or part of an old coat hanger across the top of a can. Pour the thinned urethane mixture into the can. When you dip your paint brush into the urethane, wipe both sides of the brush across the wire (Fig. 7-1). This will remove excess liquid and squeeze air bubbles out of your brush.

Apply a thin coat of urethane. Use long strokes to avoid brush marks. Be careful not to let excess urethane accumulate in grooves and crevices. When every piece of the piano has been coated with urethane, let them dry, and then apply a thin second coat. Refer to the manufacturer's directions as to how much time to allow between coats.

Keep your work area as dust-free as possible during the application of urethane and the drying time. Allow the second coat to dry completely before you handle the pieces. When the second coat of urethane is thoroughly dry, you can begin to put your piano back together.

Putting the Piano Back Together

It should be easier to put your piano back together than it was to take it apart, because you are now familiar with the various parts. Certainly it will be more satisfying to work with the lovely refinished wood.

REASSEMBLING INDIVIDUAL PIECES

Begin by removing the plastic and the rags that are covering the harp. Also remove any staples. You are now ready to reassemble your piano.

The Top Panel

Reattach all the pieces that were removed from the top panel. If there was an inset panel, put it back in and put back any latches and hinges that you removed. Refer to your diagram of the top panel as you work and be sure to replace the screws in the same holes they came out of.

The Fallboard

Refer to your diagram and to Fig. 4-21 as you reassemble the fallboard.

Cut the new nameboard felt the same length as the old one was, and use white glue to glue it to the bottom of piece #3 of the fallboard. Because the edge of the nameboard felt will show from the front of the piano, be sure you put it on straight and in the same place as the old felt was. This nameboard felt acts as a cushion for the back end of the keys so they don't make a clicking sound after you release a note.

While the glue is drying, put the front, curved piece of the fallboard and the middle section back together with the long hinge.

If you got new knobs for the fallboard, put them on now, too. New knobs sometimes have a screw protruding from the backside where the old knobs may have had wooden dowels. If this is the case, you will need to plug the hole by gluing a short piece of dowel into it. When the hole has been plugged, drill a shallow pilot hole in the center of the dowel and screw the new knob into it. The new knob will completely hide the dowel that plugs the hole.

Last, put the third piece of the fallboard back on. Use the small hinges. Set the completed fallboard aside until it is time to put it back on the piano.

The Bottom Rail

You need to replace the pieces of felt that surrounded each pedal in the openings of the bottom rail. Refer to Fig. 4-16 and to your diagram. Use the old piece of felt that you saved as patterns and cut new pieces of felt the same sizes. Don't glue the new felt on yet. First, hold the pieces in place in one pedal hole and check to see that the pedal can be reinserted with the felt in place. If the pedals will fit, go ahead and glue the new felt on at this time. If the pedals don't fit with the felt in place, set the new pieces of felt aside and wait until the pedals have been put back on before you glue on the new felt.

The Back Rail Cloth

If you are going to replace the back rail cloth, this is a good time to do it. The back rail cloth is the thick piece of felt that is on the back of the key frame. Fig. 4-7 and Fig. 4-8 will refresh your memory. If you are putting on a new back rail cloth, be sure to measure accurately so that it is the same size as the old one was.

You may only want to glue down the backside of the back rail cloth in case the front edge goes over some of the screws that hold the key frame to the key bed.

The Lid

Put the long hinge back on the top of the piano and then reattach the lid to the other side of the hinge.

Rubber Bumpers and Other Hardware

Replace the rubber bumpers in each place where you removed one. Usually, these bumpers are found in the following places:

- [ ] On top of the piano, where the open lid rests.
- [ ] On top of the key slip, where the closed fallboard rests.
- [ ] On top of the sides of the piano, where the closed lid rests.
- [ ] On top of the front piece of the fallboard, where it rests against the back piece when the fallboard is open.

Refer to your notes and diagrams to get all the rubber bumpers back in place.

Reattach any other hinges or hardware that you removed. If your piano has a lock, put the keyhole assembly back in the key slip.

REPLACING THE PEDALS

If you were able to remove the bottom rail, put it back on now. If there was a metal plate surrounding your pedals, put that back on, too. Put the pedals back through the holes in the bottom rail, keeping them in the proper order. Screw the metal or wooden blocks back on to the back ends of the pedals. (Refer to Fig. 4-15, which shows one of these blocks being removed.)

If you could not put the new felt around the pedal openings before, glue it in place at this time.

Refer back to Fig. 4-14, which shows the rocker arm and its attachments. Put the pivot pin back through the side of the rocker arm for each pedal, and then put the felt washer and nut back on the top of each rod. If the felt washers are not in good condition, you can easily make new ones using the piece of felt you ordered for miscellaneous use. Just cut a small square of felt and poke a hole in the middle of it to create a new washer. There is usually a felt washer at the bottom of each rod, also, to prevent a click of metal to metal when the pedal is used. Replace these washers with new ones, too, if necessary.

You took careful measurements of exactly how far each rod should stick up above the nut. Refer to these measurements and replace the nuts exactly as they were. Be sure you are putting these threaded rods back in the same holes in the pedals that they came out of. This information will be on the diagram you made.

ATTACHING THE KEY CHEEKS, KEY BED, AND LEGS

If you were able to remove the key cheeks from your piano,

you should put them back on now. Check to be sure you are putting the left key cheek on the left side of the piano and the right key cheek on the right side of the piano. Figure 4-20 shows the screw holes in a key cheek that was being removed.

After the key cheeks are on, replace any extra piece of wood that was originally attached to the inside of the key cheeks.

Put the key bed back in place and replace the screws that go up through the bottom of it and anchor it to the bottom of the key cheeks. If there was also a screw anchoring the key bed to the harp, replace it.

Put the legs of the piano back in place and screw them on with the screws that go down through the key bed into the top of the legs. Next put in the screws that go up through the block of wood and into the bottom of the legs. Replace the castors if you removed them.

STANDING THE PIANO UP

The piano can now be returned to its upright position. Remember, a piano is heavy and because it is on casters, it will tend to roll away from you so don't try to do this alone. Get help!

Two people should pick up the bottom of the piano just far enough for a third person to remove the two 4-×-4s. Then rest the bottom of the piano on the floor.

Now have one person stand in front of the piano to keep it from rolling. Two or three others can lift the top end of the piano off the 4-×-4s and stand it upright again.

Remove the plastic and pieces of material from the back side of the piano and discard them. Also remove all the staples.

PEDAL DOWELS, KEY FRAME, AND KEY BLOCKS

Insert the pedal dowels through the key bed and put them in to the ends of the pedal rocker arms.

Put the key frame back on the key bed. Be careful to replace any paper or wooden spacers that you found underneath the key frame when you removed it. Screw the key frame to the key bed. If necessary, finish gluing down the back rail cloth.

Put the key blocks back in place. Keep the right and left sides straight. Screw the key blocks to the key bed.

PUTTING IN THE KEYS

This part will be fun, especially if you put new key covers on your keys. At last the piano is beginning to look like a piano again!

Starting with the #1 key, on the left side, put the keys back in place, one at a time. Set them straight down on the balance rail pins and front rail pins. Be careful not to bend any of the pins.

If you replaced the key covers, you need to check to be sure that each key now works freely without rubbing on the key next to it. Sometimes the new key covers are slightly wider than the original covers were. If this is the case, the new white covers will need to be filed down. You don't need to take the key covers off in order to do this. Just remove the key and gently file down the edges a little bit and then put the key back on and try it again. Keep filing until the white key no longer scrapes against the black key when it is played.

REPLACING THE ACTION

It will take two people to put the action back in the piano. One person should stand on each end of the action, as in Fig. 3-16. Carefully put the action back into the piano, about 6 inches above the back end of the black keys. Tilt the top of the action slightly forward so that the bottom edge of the action leads the way into the piano.

When the bottom edge of the action reaches the pins that are sticking up from the key bed, put the action on these guide pins and then slowly tilt the top of the action back the last few inches so that the dampers make contact with the strings. Refer to your notes and to Chapter 3 to be sure you get the dampers positioned properly on the strings. Don't rush this part of the job. Move the action slowly and carefully until you get it in the right place.

Loosely reattach one of the knurled knobs, which fasten the action to the harp. These knurled knobs are shown in Fig. 2-7. Don't put on all of these knobs quite yet; you should put in the pedal dowels first.

PUTTING IN THE PEDAL DOWELS

The tops of the pedal dowels should now be reattached to the action. Refer to your sketch to get them in the right place. The action may need to be lifted slightly to allow the ends of the pedal dowels to fit. Be careful not to bend any of the dampers.

If the damper rail cannot be lifted far enough to get the pedal dowels reattached, you can remove the lower end of the pedal dowels from the rocker arms. Then you can put the upper end of the pedal dowels on the action and then go back and reattach the bottom of the pedal dowel by pushing down on the rocker arm to give yourself some space.

When the pedal dowels have been reattached, replace the rest of the knurled knobs that fasten the action to the harp and firmly tighten them, by hand only.

Try the pedals to be sure they work the same way they did before you took them apart. If there is too much play in the pedals, or not enough play, you can make a slight adjustment by screwing the nut up or down at the top of the bolt that attaches the back of the pedal to the rocker arm. Even though you made accurate measurements here, some adjustment may be necessary in order to get the pedals working the way they should.

KEY SLIP, BOTTOM PANEL, AND FALLBOARD

Put the key slip back in place and screw it in from the bottom. This is another place where new white key covers sometimes cause a problem. If the size of your new key covers makes the front edge of the keys hit the key slip when the piano is played, slightly loosen the key slip screws and slide the key slip forward about one-sixteenth of an inch. Put a small piece of shim between the front of the key block and the key slip on both sides. A business card folded in half is about the right size and thickness.

Push the key slip back tight, leaving the shims there, and tighten the key slip screws. The pieces of shim will cause the key slip to be slightly farther forward than it was and thus will keep the new key covers from hitting it.

Replace the bottom panel by tilting the top of it toward you and guiding the bottom of it on to the wooden dowels. Fasten it with the latch or whatever mechanism secures it.

Attach the reassembled fallboard to the back side of the key blocks.

MUSIC SHELF, TOP PILLARS, AND TOP PANEL

Put the music shelf back in place and screw it on. If you were able to remove the top pillars, replace them. Be sure to keep track of right and left, as well as top and bottom. When the top pillars are back on, replace the top panel and secure it to the frame.

CONGRATULATE YOURSELF

That's it! Your piano is now completely refinished and can be moved to its place of honor in your home. This would be a good time to have the piano tuned—and don't forget to take your "after" photo.

Give yourself a pat on the back for a job well done. You can enjoy your beautiful piano for many years, and you deserve all the compliments you are sure to receive on its new appearance.

Appendix

SUPPLIERS

Pacific Piano Supply Co.
11323 Van Owen Street
P.O. Box 9412
North Hollywood, CA 91609
(818) 877-0674

Player Piano Co., Inc.
620 East Douglas
Wichita, KS 67202
(316) 263-3241

Schaff Piano Supply Co.
2009-21 North Clybourn Avenue
Chicago, IL 60614
(312) 477-7220

Index

Index

OTHER POPULAR TAB BOOKS OF INTEREST